A Preface to

RESTORATION DRAMA

* * *

A Preface to Restoration Drama

* * *

JOHN HAROLD WILSON

HARVARD UNIVERSITY PRESS
CAMBRIDGE, MASSACHUSETTS
1968

Distributed in Great Britain by Oxford University Press, London

This book was first published
by Houghton Mifflin Company in
Riverside Studies in Literature
(Gordon N. Ray, General Editor)

PRINTED IN THE UNITED STATES OF AMERICA

Foreword

* * *

THE PURPOSE of this essay is to introduce students of the drama to one of the great periods of English dramatic activity, the Restoration Age—from the return of King Charles II in 1660 to the accession of Queen Anne in 1702. In the past, many critics and literary historians have undervalued Restoration drama, and some have vilified it for its "immorality." But in recent years the tide of taste has turned, and the modern tendency has been to overvalue and to read profound meanings and symbolisms into the tragedies and comedies of the period. I confess that, after a lifetime spent reading, re-reading, and pondering over a considerable body of drama, one tends to become its advocate. Nevertheless, in the following pages I have tried to define and describe the varieties of Restoration drama and to analyze outstanding examples of each kind objectively, without bias or prejudice. In any dramatic period—even in the Renaissance—comparatively few plays out of the thousands in print repay the curious reader. But in the desert of the past there are enough lush oases to make a visit to the Restoration stage pleasant and profitable.

Since this is a "preface" to Restoration drama, my examens of selected plays are necessarily brief, and my conclusions tentative; every generation must evaluate its literary heritage according to its own standards. Wherever possible, I have chosen to deal with plays readily accessible in modern editions. To avoid confusion, I have normalized the spelling and punctuation of all quoted passages. The production dates of plays appear in parentheses after the titles. When the reference is to a preface or dedication, the publication date appears; if the publication date is later than the date of production, it appears prefaced by "printed in." For all dates I have followed *The London Stage, 1660–1700,* edd. Avery, Scouten, and Van Lennep, Carbondale, Illinois, 1965.

For many useful suggestions and for painstaking reading and criticism, I am deeply indebted to Professor Richard D. Altick and Louise Walker Wilson.

J. H. W.

Contents

* * *

A Preface to

RESTORATION DRAMA

* * *

*** *1* ***

Prologue

EARLY ON THE MORNING of May 25, 1660, the beaches of Dover were black with people watching Admiral Montagu's little fleet as it glided into the harbor and anchored. From the flagship, about noon, a barge walked over the water on shining oars. It grated on the shingle, the guns in forts and ships belched flame and smoke, the crowd roared its welcome, and King Charles II, a tall, swarthy man with sensual lips and cynical eyes, stepped ashore, knelt, and thanked God for his miraculous return to his native land.

For eighteen years, since the breaking out of civil war between King Charles I and his Parliament, young Charles Stuart had endured war, defeat, flight, exile, humiliation, poverty, and hunger. They were years marked by his retreat to the Scilly Isles after the defeat of the royalist army at Naseby; by the capture, imprisonment, trial, and execution of his worthless father on January 20, 1649; by the setting up of an English republic; by the young King's defeat at the battle of Worcester on September 3, 1651, and his romantic escape, during which he had spent a long day hiding in a hollow oak near Boscobel; by Cromwell's seizure of power as Lord Protector, his death in

1658, and General Monk's summons to a Convention Parliament, which, in turn, had invited Charles, then a miserable exile in Holland, to return to his kingdom — to forgive and forget. He forgave, but he never forgot.

On May 29 (the King's thirtieth birthday), "with a triumph of above 20,000 horse and foot, brandishing their swords and shouting with inexpressible joy; the ways strewed with flowers, the bells ringing, the streets hung with tapestries, fountains running wine," Charles II rode through ecstatic London to Whitehall, the palace of his ancestors. The new age which began that day is commonly called the Restoration, because it marked the restoration of King, Parliament, the hereditary upper classes, and the Anglican Church to power to the state. It is a catchall title for the years from 1660 to the reign of Queen Anne, a period which includes three reigns: King Charles II (1660–1685), James II (1685–1689), and William and Mary (1689–1702). The Restoration marked the end of a premature experiment in republicanism, maintained by bayonets. It marked also the end of Puritan laws against holidays, plays, music, dancing, outdoor games, and such indoor sports as dice, cards and wenching. At the Restoration, the lid came off; England was merry again; the sons of Belial came out of hiding and danced in the streets, "flown with insolence and wine."

The Restoration was an age of conflict and contradiction. Sometimes called the beginning of the Enlightenment, it prided itself upon its reasonableness, and yet was marred by ignorance, brutality, and blind hatred. It claimed culture and civilization, but it whipped prostitutes, imprisoned debtors, hanged and disemboweled criminals, and burned women at the stake. It was an age which had inherited the scientific discoveries of Copernicus, Kepler, Bacon, Galileo, Harvey, Gilbert, and Torricelli, an age which produced Newton, Boyle, Hooke, and the Royal Society — and yet it trembled at the appearance of "a blazing star," a comet. It was a liberty-loving age which gave birth to the Habeas Corpus Act, but which persecuted Catholics and Nonconformists, suppressed unlicensed books, and hanged priests. It was a prosperous age for merchants and landowners, yet it was plagued by slums, poverty, beggars, thieves, and highwaymen. Although in the upper levels of society it was an age of luxury and refinement, its cities were filthy, rat-infested, and diseased. It was an age which is sometimes considered the beginning of modern times because it established standing armies and navies, banks, banknotes, milled coinage — and a national debt.

To the average man, who cared very little whether the sun went around the earth or vice versa, or whether his blood circulated in his veins or, like a "standing lake," boiled up into a flood in the course of a fever, the two important conflicts of his age were religious and political. Passionately Protestant, the average man clung to the Established Church with the King as its titular head, and hated almost equally the authoritarian right and the radical left. He feared the power of Roman Catholicism, especially as it was represented by Louis XIV of France, who sought to bring all Europe under his sway and back to the mother church. Remembering the fires of Smithfield, the Gunpowder Plot (which he celebrated every November 5 with fireworks and the burning of guys and popes), and the Irish massacres of 1641, the average man lived in daily apprehension of a domestic foe. Therefore he demanded enforcement of the laws which required Catholics to attend Anglican services, forbade the practice of their religion, and proscribed priests. National fear reached its apogee in 1678, when Titus Oates, a talented liar, came forth with his wild tale of a Popish Plot to kill King Charles and put all Protestants to the sword. For nearly four years all England woke, worked, and slept with fear.

But the average man dreaded also the radical left: the outwardly conforming Puritans, who wished to cleanse the Anglican Church of its popish practices, and the nonconforming Puritans (or "fanatics"), who refused to follow the legally prescribed forms of worship. The latter he feared as rebels who sought to undermine the foundations of church and state. He demanded restrictive laws against Presbyterians, Independents, Baptists, Quakers, and such splinter sects as Unitarians, Seekers, Antinomians, Fifth Monarchists, Adamites, Ranters, and the Family of Love. By imposing various tests, the average man virtually limited public officeholding to Anglicans. Even the Toleration Act of 1689, which officially recognized Nonconformists, or Dissenters, merely declared that the penal laws against them would not be enforced if they took oaths of fidelity to William and Mary and disclaimed the doctrine of transubstantiation. For the Catholics, the Act did nothing at all.

Because the Anglicans and the Catholics were, in the main, royalists, and the Nonconformists were usually republicans, religious and political conflicts were practically inseparable. The political conflict involved the slow and often painful process by which near-absolute monarchy was becoming limited, constitutional monarchy. Kings tried to cling to their prerogatives, and Parliaments tore them away one by one. From James I, who claimed to rule by divine right, to William III, who knew very well that he owed his crown to Parliament, stretched eighty years of discord, tumult, and civil strife.

There was very little peace for the average man. All through the last half of the century he was plagued by war, rumors of war, and fear of invasion by Dutch, French, or rebel forces. Great Britain was no longer safe in her sea-girt isles. In the second Dutch War (1665–1667), battles at sea were bloody but inconclusive, and in the spring of 1667 the Dutch fleet sailed up the Medway, burned a number of warships at anchor, and towed away the *Royal Charles,* the English flagship. The event climaxed two years of disaster: the Great Plague of 1665, which killed 68,000 people in London alone, and the Great Fire of September, 1666, which destroyed nearly all the old City proper. The third Dutch War (1672–1674) was as indecisive as the second. England gained nothing by its long, costly wars with its great trade rival.

In June, 1685, James, Duke of Monmouth (King Charles's oldest illegitimate son), invaded southern England, declared himself king as the true successor to his father, and gathered an army which was destroyed at the battle of Sedgemoor in July.

In November, 1688, at the invitation of leading Whigs, William of Orange landed a powerful Dutch army in southern England; James II fled to France; and a convention parliament named William and his wife Mary (James's daughter) as joint sovereigns. Then came eight years of exhausting war with France, ending with the Treaty of Ryswick in 1697. After five years of calm came eleven more years of bloody campaigning on the continent in the War of the Spanish Succession.

Between wars, England prospered, and the average man found time and money for many pleasures. He cared little for literature. In general, the Nonconformists and Puritans disapproved of non-didactic literature and read only sermons, tracts, and polemics. But two great Puritan poets, Andrew Marvell and John Milton, continued to flourish in the Restoration age. Most of Marvell's satires were written after 1660, and Milton's *Paradise Lost, Paradise Regained,* and *Samson Agonistes* were published in the years 1667–1671. And we must not forget the Baptist preacher John Bunyan, who wrote two great didactic narratives in jail, *Grace Abounding* (1666) and *The Pilgrim's Progress* (1678).

Ladies and gentlemen read poetry, essays, and plays. After Marvell and Milton, the chief Restoration poets were Waller, Cowley, Dryden, Rochester, Butler, Oldham, and Prior. It was a great age for songs, especially for persuasion-to-love lyrics, which a host of minor poets turned out by the thousand. Because of the age's emphasis on rationalism, which shows vividly the contrast between what is and what might be, it was also a great age for satire; notable examples are Butler's *Hudibras,* Rochester's *Satire against Mankind,* Dryden's *Religio Laici* and *Absalom and Achitophel,* and Defoe's *The True-born Englishman.* In a world which turned its eyes inward for self-analysis, it is appropriate that two famous diarists flourished, Samuel Pepys and John Evelyn. Political writings abounded, from Thomas Hobbes's absolutist *Leviathan* (1652) to John Locke's liberal *Discourses on Government* (1690).

The Restoration's chief claim to literary consideration, however, is its drama: the heroic tragedies of Dryden, the sensational plays of Lee, the pathos and terror of Otway, the broad "humors" of Shadwell and Ravenscroft, the satire of Wycherley, and the witty comedies of Etherege and Congreve. Because of its drama, the Restoration has long been considered the most immoral of all modern periods. It was not. Reacting against Puritan hypocrisy and encouraged by the scandalous example of King Charles and his Court, it was simply more open, more brazen, in its immorality. The chances are that there were no more sinners per thousand in the days of the Merry Monarch than in the straitlaced reign of Queen Victoria.

Restoration drama reflected its period. Unlike other forms of narrative art, a play, to be successful, must be written to give immediate pleasure to a sizable audience. A novel can make its way to success over months or even years, but a play must hit or perish. Consequently a popular play in any age is a good index to the tastes and attitudes of the audience for which it was written. When we read a Restoration play, then, we have to see it, first, in terms of its date, through the eyes of its immediate audience — the small coterie of cultivated gentry who supported the Restoration theater. A play is the product of four factors: playwright, actors, stage, and audience.

As it appears on the printed page, any play is more than a scenario but less than a complete production. Like a musical score played by musicians, a play is complete when it is performed on a stage before an audience. But the skilled reader can produce a play in his imagination. Like the musician who can read a score and enjoy the sweetness of unheard melodies, the reader of a printed play can set his stage, cast his characters, and watch the progress of the play with his mind's eye. The more his knowledge and skill, the greater his pleasure.

With a modern play the process is comparatively easy, especially if the reader is a frequent playgoer, acquainted with the ways of the contemporary stage and the methods of actors. With a play written in the Restoration period, the process is difficult. A typical Restoration play is a book of fifty to sixty quarto pages, which was offered for sale, sewn and without covers, for sixpence; it was, in effect, a paperback, convenient for a daring young girl to hide under her pillow. It consists of a title page, followed by a servile dedication to some great lord or lady, a prologue, the dramatis personae (sometimes with the names of the players who created the roles), the text of a five-act play with the acts and scenes numbered, and an epilogue. Occasionally there is a critical or personal preface, and sometimes the characters are briefly analyzed in the dramatis personae. Usually that is all.

In a typical Restoration play, stage directions are often no more than the customary "Enter," "Exit," and "Aside," and settings are labeled only as "A Street," "The New Exchange," "A Temple," "A Camp," or somebody's "House," "Lodgings," or "Bedroom." There are none of the elaborate directions about stage properties and business and the detailed descriptions of scenes and people which make modern plays so easy to visualize. Moreover the (to us) naive conventions of the Restoration stage and the formalized methods of the players were radically unlike those we are accustomed to. To produce on the modern stage — even in imagination — a play written for a Restoration theater is like playing on a saxophone music written for a harpsichord. In addition, Restoration playwrights were writing for repertory companies of players, whose abilities and specialties strongly affected the writer's product. Finally, the playwrights — called "poets" by their contemporaries — were writing for audiences whose experiences, attitudes, and tastes differed widely from ours.

It follows, then, that before we can visualize and enjoy a Restoration play we must strike up an acquaintance with the Restoration theater, the actors, the audiences, and the playwrights.

*** 2 ***

The Restoration Theater

ON SEPTEMBER 2, 1642, at the beginning of the Civil War, the edict of a Puritan Parliament closed all the theaters in London "to appease and avert the wrath of God." Nevertheless, all through the Interregnum, bands of players defied the wrath of both God and Parliament, and produced plays from time to time under great difficulties. To enforce its edict, in 1644 Parliament had the Globe Theater pulled down, ostensibly to make room for tenements. In 1649 it sent soldiers to wreck the interiors of the Fortune, Cockpit, and Salisbury Court theaters (the Fortune was finally demolished in 1662). In 1655 it ordered the famous Blackfriars pulled down, again to make room for tenements. By 1660 most of the great Elizabethan theaters, with their sceneless platform stages, had disappeared, and the smaller survivors were shabby, noisy, and outmoded.

Two new companies of players, the King's and the Duke's, were organized in November, 1660, dividing a theatrical monopoly for all London. The King's Company played briefly at the old Red Bull in St. John's Street, and then moved to Gibbons' Tennis Court in Vere Street, which was fitted out with a bare platform stage. The Duke's Company played in the Salisbury Court Theater while remodeling Lisle's Tennis Court in Lincoln's Inn Fields and building a stage equipped with scenes. The King's Company put all its money and energies into building a fine new theater in Bridges Street, near Drury Lane. It cost £2,400, but it had a modern stage and all the latest inventions in scenes and machines.

On Thursday, May 7, 1663, the new Theater Royal (ancestor of the Drury Lane Theater) opened its doors for the first time. Notices of the opening, with the title of the play to be performed, were tacked to posts about London. Among those who saw the bills was Mr. Samuel Pepys, Clerk of the Acts of the Navy. A merry little man and very fond of plays, Mr. Pepys was eager to see the new theater, but he was too busy on the opening day. Soon after dinner on Friday he took his wife and her maid by coach along Fleet Street, the Strand, and up Drury Lane to Playhouse Yard, the entry to the Theater Royal.

At the outer door of the big brick-and-timber building, Mr. Pepys paid seven shillings and sixpence (2/6 apiece), receiving in exchange three round metal tokens. He led his ladies through a passageway (which struck him as too narrow) into the ground floor pit, which sloped from the rear boxes down to the stage and provided backless benches covered with matting for seats. At the entrance to the pit Mr. Pepys surrendered his tokens to a doorkeeper. It was still early, and the three had no trouble finding good seats in the middle of the pit — there were no reserved seats anywhere in the house. Mr. Pepys looked about him with somewhat qualified satisfaction. The shadowy house was nearly twice the size of Gibbons' Tennis Court. It was well-built, ornate, and completely roofed in, with a windowed cupola atop to let in the daylight, and sometimes cold winds, rain, and hail. But today was mild; there was no need to sit wrapped in one's cloak until the animal heat of the spectators warmed the auditorium. There were places for — at a guess — five hundred people. The forestage, carpeted with green baize, jutted its oval bulk well out into the pit in front of the elaborately carved and gilded proscenium arch, which spanned the inside width of the theater. Over the forestage hung rings, or chandeliers, of wax candles, which the candle-snuffer was already lighting. (Oil lamps for footlights came in a few years later.)

Before the play began the proscenium curtains were closed, of course, but the two doors on each side of the forestage (in front of and at right angles to the proscenium arch) were open; above each door was a window. (If Mr. Pepys had looked sharply, he could have seen Charles Booth, the prompter, standing inside a doorway with his book in his hand and a bell for signaling scene changes attached to one wrist.)

Around three sides of the house, the boxes (four shillings) were gradually filling with ladies and gentlemen of wealth and fashion. Above the boxes were the middle galleries (eighteen pence) for lesser folk, and above them the upper galleries (a shilling) for servants and apprentices. As Mr. Pepys finished his survey, he admitted to himself that the house was made "with extraordinary good contrivance," but he shook his head at the distance from the stage to the rear boxes, "which," he said, "I am confident cannot hear." Yet the outside dimension of the building was only about 112 by 58 feet, and the distance from the stage to the rear boxes was less than thirty feet.

When the orchestra struck up the First Music, Mr. Pepys, a true music lover, was further disquieted: "the music being below" the level of the pit, instead of in a music room over the proscenium arch, "and most of it sounding under the very stage, there is no hearing of the basses at all, nor very well of the trebles, which sure must be mended." Of course, with the orange girls now bawling their wares in the pit — sixpence for a small China orange — few could enjoy the First Music anyway, and as the pit, boxes, and galleries filled with chattering people, fewer still could hear the Second Music.

Mr. Pepys, who had a sharp eye for beauty, amused himself by watching the people who drifted into the pit. He had no program to read. None was needed; everybody knew the old play announced for today, and everybody knew the "old and excellent actors" who were to perform it. Mr. Pepys decided that all the ladies he saw were "finer and better dressed in the pit than they used . . . to be." As the house filled, some of them donned vizard masks, "which of late is become a great fashion among the ladies." Very soon the vizard mask was to become the mark of the prowling prostitute.

At half-past three the house settled down, the Third Music (the "curtain tune") came to an end, an actor spoke a pretty prologue to laughter and applause, and the curtains rose — to remain open until after the epilogue. Behind the proscenium arch appeared a palace scene painted on a pair of closed wing screens (tall, sliding flats). The first players strode on-stage through one of the forestage doors, and the play began. It was John Fletcher's old romantic comedy, *The Humorous Lieutenant,* "a play," grumbled Mr. Pepys, "that hath little good in it, nor much in the very part, which, by the King's command, Lacy now acts instead of Clun" — the comic Lieutenant. But, on the whole, the play was pleasant enough, and at the end of every act the stage cleared, and the musicians played a minuet, a jig, or a coranto. Mr. Pepys found some good things worth commenting on: "in the dance, the tall devil's actions was very pretty." At last the play ended, an actor spoke the epilogue, the curtains fell, another actor announced the next day's play, the music struck up again, and Mr. Pepys and his family went home.

It is too bad that Mr. Pepys failed to describe the scenes for *The Humorous Lieutenant,* which must have been new and striking. Probably Sir William Davenant's "Opera" — the Duke's Theater in Lisle's Tennis Court, where scenes were already in use — had made him blasé. In the new Theater Royal the proscenium arch split the depth of the stage into two nearly equal parts. Behind the arch, in the "scene" area, four large, well-spaced pairs of wing flats, or shutters (usually wooden frames covered with painted canvas), opened and closed according to the settings demanded by the play. They slid in grooves across the stage, closing to represent painted houses, rooms, streets, and landscapes, and opening ("drawing") to disclose still deeper scenes or to "discover" players in various postures, situations, or tableaux. Cut-out flats with openings to show distant views gave the illusion of greater depth. All the wing flats could be opened wide to present a perspective leading to a scene painted on the back shutter at the full depth of the stage. The players moved easily from the scene area to the forestage and back again, usually entering and leaving by the forestage doors, but they could step directly from one scene to another without leaving the stage. Within the scene area they could climb "practical" (i.e., solid or substantial) trees, walls, or battlements, sit on chairs at dressing or gaming tables, and lie in canopied beds.

In the next few years Mr. Pepys became well acquainted with all the ins and outs of the King's Theater and with most of its personnel, from Tom Killigrew, the King's Jester and Master of the company, to Orange Moll, the fruitwoman and queen of the orange girls. Once while the playhouse was closed during the Great Plague (from June, 1665, to November, 1666), he visited the building, which was "all in dirt, they being altering of the stage to make it wider." He took advantage of the situation to wander alone backstage. Illusion vanished when he visited the tiring rooms above the scene area. "But to see their clothes, and the various sorts, and what a mixture of things there was; here a wooden leg, there a ruff, here a hobby-horse, there a crown, would make a man split himself to see with laughing; and particularly Lacy's wardrobe and Shottrells! But then again, to think how fine [the clothes] show on the stage by candle-light, and how poor things they are to look now too near hand, is not pleasant at all." But the machines were very fine, and the stores of painted scenes "very pretty."

During the plague year Mr. Pepys became intimate with Elizabeth Knepp, a pretty little singer and actress at the Theater Royal, married to "a kind of a jockey." She was a great source of theatrical gossip and an excellent guide to the backstage. Once she found Mr. and Mrs. Pepys in the pit after a play was over and took them through the pit door backstage, where they met and kissed pretty, witty Nell Gwyn, the rising young comedienne. Afterward Mrs. Knepp made them stay in a side-box and watch a rehearsal of the dances for the next day's play. "And so away thence, pleased with this sight also, and specially kissing of Nell."

On a later occasion Mrs. Knepp met them before the play began, "and," said Mr. Pepys, "she took us up into the tiring rooms and to the women's shift, where Nell was dressing herself, and was all unready" — dressed only in her smock — "and is very pretty, prettier than I thought." The women's shift was the dressing room for actresses, but the ladies of the stage had no particular modesty and cheerfully admitted male visitors. Through a little window the players could look down into the auditorium and estimate the day's attendance. "But to see how Nell cursed, for having so few people in the pit, was pretty." A small audience meant a different play for the next afternoon, and a laborious morning of rehearsals. "And so [we] walked all up and down the house above [the scene area], and then below to the scene-room, and [Mrs. Knepp] gave us fruit; and here I read the questions to Knepp, which she answered me, all through her part of 'Flora's Figaries' which was acted today. But, Lord! to see how they were both painted would make a man mad, and did make me loath them; and what base company of men comes among them, and how lewdly they talk! and how poor [the actors] are in clothes, and yet what a show they make on the stage by candle-light, is very observable. . . . By and by into the pit, and there saw the play [Rhodes's *Flora's Vagaries,* 1663], which was pretty good, but my belly was full of what I had seen in the house."

Because Mr. Pepys, whose eyes were failing, closed his diary in June, 1669, he left us no description of the splendid new Duke's Theater in Dorset Garden, fronting on the Thames. Built at a cost estimated at £9,000, it opened its doors on November 9, 1671. In structure it was much like the first Theater Royal in Bridges Street, but it was larger, more richly decorated, and equipped with more elaborate machines. The unlucky King's Company lost its playhouse by fire on the night of January 26, 1672, and for two years while it rebuilt, it had to make do with

Lisle's Tennis Court, recently vacated by the Duke's Company. The second Theater Royal in Bridges Street was again smaller than its rival. A "plain-built house" which cost about £4,000, it opened on March 26, 1674. Until the end of the century the King's and the Duke's remained the chief popular playhouses. In 1682 the Duke's Company swallowed up the remnants of the failing King's Players, and the new United Company kept both theaters in use: the Dorset Garden Theater for spectacles and operas, the Theater Royal for less demanding plays.

Regrettably, Mr. Pepys never set down for us the information Mrs. Knepp gave him one evening about "the whole practices of the playhouse and players," an account which would have been worth her weight in gold. For the practices and conventions of the Restoration stage, we have to turn to many sources in addition to Mr. Pepys — chiefly to the plays themselves.

The Restoration inherited a great deal from the Elizabethan stage, and many earlier practices designed for realistic effects continued almost without change. Thus, for example, when a storm was to be represented, one scenekeeper (stage hand) rolled a cannon ball over sticks backstage or rolled and pounded a wooden mustard bowl, while another scenekeeper flashed pans of gunpowder, squibs, or powdered rosin in a tube, and a musician rumbled a bass drum. Again, the theaters kept on hand a supply of blunted swords for duels, and of blunted or collapsible daggers for murders and suicides. These were not accident proof. In 1673 Philip Cademan, of the Duke's Company, dueling with Henry Harris on the stage, "was unfortunately with a sharp foil pierced near the eye, which so maimed both his hand and speech" that he was incapable of acting thereafter. In 1692 Samuel Sandford and George Powell were acting in Dryden and Lee's *Oedipus*. By mistake Sandford picked up "a sharp dagger for one that runs the blade into the handle," and stabbed Powell, who came very close to dying in earnest. Again, before a performance of Lee's *The Rival Queens*, Mrs. Barry and Mrs. Boutell quarreled over the ownership of a scarf and went onstage still angry. In the course of the play Mrs. Barry stabbed

Mrs. Boutell with a property dagger; she "struck with such force that though the point of the dagger was blunted it made its way through Mrs. Boutell's stays and entered about a quarter of an inch in the flesh."

Just as on the Elizabethan stage, wounds were imitated by dollops of fresh sheep's blood, applied to the face or body by a well-soaked sponge tied inside the player's hand or contained in a bladder against his body, to be broken by the blow of a sword. Actors were wounded, tortured, and racked in full view of the audience, where their screams could be heard and their agonized faces clearly seen. Mimic victims died on-stage, but usually within the scene area so that concealing flats could close, and the actors could get up and walk off under their own power. If an actor died on the forestage, bearers picked him up and lugged him off on a stretcher.

Although the stage was illuminated by daylight, chandeliers, and footlights, darkness on-stage was still indicated by bringing on lighted candles, lanterns, or torches. When such lights were put out, the players groped about the stage in purely imaginary blackness. Stage conventions of this kind are rarely noticed or challenged by playgoers accustomed to them. Once, however, when Kynaston was unable to play and Beeston read his part, Mr. Pepys commented, "But it was pleasant to see Beeston come in with others, supposing it to be dark, and yet he is forced to read his part by the light of the candles; and this I observing to a gentleman that sat by me, he was mightily pleased therewith, and spread it up and down" through the pit.

By appealing to the spectator's imagination, the poets could make the forestage doors represent anything they chose: closet doors, bedroom doors, cell doors, or outside house doors with the windows above serving as balconies or as entrances to upper floors. The doors were large enough to admit horses; at a performance of Shirley's *Hyde Park* in the King's House, Mr. Pepys saw horses brought upon the stage. In 1697 the comedian Jo Haynes made theatrical history by delivering a prologue from the back of an ass.

Of course there were trap doors in the forestage as there had been in the Elizabethan theaters, for ghosts and spirits to make their sudden appearances, and for devils to rise from Hell and sink back laden with lost souls. But now there were trap doors within the scene area also. Some of these were so large, and the machines in the cellarage so powerful, that whole structures could be made to rise from below or sink into the depths. In the flies above the scene area, a variety of complex machines, attended by skilled machinists and worked by scenekeepers toiling at ropes and windlasses, could send witches flying through the air, lift gods and goddesses to Olympus, lower clouds filled with singers, and cause large illuminated suns and moons to rise or set.

Although scenes had been used in Court masques before 1642, the use of painted wings and shutters was a novelty in the public theaters. The scenes were elaborate and decorative. They ran the gamut of pictorial backgrounds, from romantic grottoes, caves, woods, and castles to sharply realistic pictures of well-known London scenes. Most of the scenery could be used over and over in many different plays. Occasionally special scenes were painted for a new play (in oil or distemper), at considerable expense. The sliding wings gave the playwright freedom to change his settings quickly and as often as he wished, without slowing the flow of action, and the complexity of stage machines gave him the means for all kinds of spectacular effects. Here, for example, are two stage directions from Dryden's opera, *Albion and Albanius* (1685):

> *The clouds divide, and Juno appears in a machine drawn by peacocks; while a symphony is playing, it moves gently forward and as it descends, it opens and discovers the tail of the peacock, which is so large that it almost fills the opening of the stage between scene and scene.*

> *A machine rises out of the sea; it opens and discovers Venus and Albanius sitting in a great scallop-shell richly adorned. Venus is attended by the Loves and Graces, Albanius by*

Heroes; the shell is drawn by dolphins. It moves forward, while a symphony of flutes-doux, etc., is playing, till it lands them on the stage, and then it closes and sinks.

The costumes for singers and dancers in an opera were always fantastic, colorful, and expensive. But for the ordinary run of plays, the Restoration merely continued the practice of earlier theaters. Any play, no matter where or when its setting, could be adequately performed in contemporary dress — the actor in full flowing periwig and wide-brimmed hat, long coat, lace cravat, flowered waistcoast, breeches cut to the fashion, shoes and stockings; the actress in any "French gown à-la-mode," with deep decolletage and the skirt looped back below the waist to show the topmost of several laced petticoats. Costumes for the players were supplied by the company, but the men had to provide their own periwigs, hats, shoes, and stockings, and the women were responsible for petticoats, gloves, shoes, stockings, and scarves. Under their costumes the men wore shirts and drawers; the women wore loose smocks falling to the knees (dancers added linen drawers). Men described as appearing "naked" on the stage actually wore shirts and drawers; women in an "undress" wore dressing gowns over their smocks.

The tiring rooms were stocked with fine clothes, most of them made by the theaters' tailors and tirewomen; some of them were discarded garments bestowed by gracious lords — even by King Charles himself. The usual materials were colorful serges, silks, and velvets, but for silver and gold lace the players had to substitute tinsel and copper-lace, which looked exceedingly rich by candle-light. The tiring rooms contained also, as Mr. Pepys discovered, a variety of exotic costumes and properties which were used more for color and show than for historical or geographical verisimilitude. There were royal robes equally appropriate for Bajazet, Cyrus the Great, Julius Caesar, and Henry the Eighth; brass crowns set with imitation jewels for kings and emperors; a set of "Roman shapes," close-fitting tunics, with capes and buskins; buff jerkins and red breeches for soldiers;

Moorish robes and turbans; clerical costumes with shovel hats; friar's robes; gowns for aldermen, lawyers, and doctors; black periwigs for murderers; blonde periwigs for women disguised as men; Elizabethan trunk hose for girls disguised as pages (the better to show off their legs); a "forest of feathers" for a hero's hat or helmet; a gilded staff or truncheon for a general; false beards, mustachios, and noses; and habits for beggars, Puritans, prelates, sailors, scholars, Irishmen, Scots, Spaniards, and Indians. Almost any mixture of costumes could be used in a given play, without concern for either accuracy or consistency. If the stage picture was beautiful and exciting, the audience was satisfied.

Such a confusing mixture of garments — especially in a society which by law or custom decreed the dress appropriate to classes and occupations — made the convention of stage disguise simple and plausible. Two girls in vizard masks, which covered their faces, had only to trade petticoats in order to exchange identities; a chimney sweep dressed as a count was accepted at his tailor's valuation; an Englishman could wear a turban, blacken his face, and become a Moor; a waiting-maid in her lady's dress could gull a gentleman into marriage; and anyone could put on a doctor's gown, look grave, carry a urinal, and cure the sick by thousands. Without the naive acceptance of disguise by dress, many Restoration plays would crumble into nonsense. As with most stage conventions of the time, the appeal was to the imagination of the audience, which found its pleasure in being well deceived.

John Dryden, the greatest playwright of the age, summed up his stage in a sentence: "In a playhouse everything contributes to impose upon the judgment; the lights, the scenes, the habits, and, above all, the grace of action, which is commonly the best where there is most need of it, surprise the audience and cast a mist upon their understandings." Generously he added, "But these false beauties of the stage are no more lasting than a rainbow; when the actor ceases to shine upon them, when he gilds them no longer with his reflection, they vanish in a twinkling."

*** 3 ***

The Players

IN THE AUTUMN of 1660, when Thomas Killigrew and Sir William Davenant received their "patents" from the King, divided their theatrical monopoly, and set up rival companies, they revived an ancient custom. The Lord Chamberlain of the Household (Edward, Earl of Manchester) swore the members of Killigrew's (the King's) company into the royal service as grooms of the great chamber in ordinary without fee (but with livery), and the members of Davenant's (the Duke's) company as grooms to the King's younger brother and heir presumptive, James, Duke of York. Thus both troupes came under the Lord Chamberlain's authority and protection, and no player in either company could be impressed into the army or navy, arrested for a misdemeanor, or sued for debt without his august permission. This arrangement suited the players, who could cheerfully run into debt, but the canny managers had another purpose in mind. Backed by the Lord Chamberlain, they became petty autocrats. No player could move from one company to another — or even to the Smock Alley troupe in Dublin — without the Lord Chamberlain's permission. The wages of hirelings — players who owned no shares in the company — were fixed and standardized. Apprentice players were required to work "three months without salary by way of approbation." Actors, even master players, or shareholders, had to play the parts assigned to them by the Master of the company or his deputy. The Lord Chamberlain could have drunken or riotous players arrested by a King's messenger, imprisoned in the Gatehouse at Whitehall, and even whipped; and the manager of either company could discharge any player at will.

From all the players available in 1660, Killigrew chose "the old men," actors in their thirties and forties — Hart, Mohun, Shatterall, Wintershall, Clun, Lacy, and others, who had learned their trade in the public theaters before the civil wars. In addition, he annexed a promising young actor, Edward Kynaston, an excellent female impersonator. Davenant got "the young men," Betterton, Underhill, Nokes, Turner, Angel, Dixon, and half a dozen more who were just learning their trade. Both companies started acting with these groups as nuclei, meanwhile hastily recruiting new actors and new "servants" for their playhouses — scenekeepers, doorkeepers, wardrobe keepers, machinists, carpenters, tailors, barbers, tirewomen, and musicians.

Almost at once the two companies discovered that they must hire women to play female roles. There were no trained boys available; there were only a few female impersonators; the old Puritan prohibition against women on the stage no longer prevailed; and many cavaliers in the audience had seen and liked the acting of women on the French and Italian stages. From dancing schools and singing schools came bevies of eager beauties. Wenches in petticoats and breeches brought lustre to the stage and new interest to the old plays in which boys had played female roles. The ladies also brought new problems to playwrights and producers. To keep them under control the managers had them sworn in also, as royal "comoedians." Then, to make a clean sweep, a year or so later they had all the theaters' servants sworn in. Now everybody who worked for a theater in any capacity — even a playwright under contract — was a sworn comedian. The members of the two companies were not serfs; they could always take up another trade.

Many of the actors were decent and respectable men who took their craft seriously, saved their money, bought houses, and raised families. Some of the actresses were respectable too; especially those married to actors, playwrights, tradesmen, and country gentlemen. The older actors, who owned shares in a company and sometimes in a theater building as well, were responsible men, well aware that their profits depended upon the company's success. In the Restoration's early years it was rumored that they were growing wealthy. Mr. Pepys reported, "I do see the gallants do begin to be tired with the vanity and pride of the theater actors, who are indeed grown very proud and rich." Their putative prosperity was short-lived but the myth lingered on. In 1681, a disgruntled poet scored them in *Poeta De Tristibus, or The Poet's Complaint:*

> The players, who scarce know to write
> Their names, or spell one word a-right,
> Or read their parts, unless writ fair
> In a large Roman character,
> Call us their slaves, who for their gain
> Must toil, and all their faults sustain.
> In gay attire each day they shine,
> Eat well, and drink the richest wine;
> All fat and plump, except some few
> The Frenchman [i.e., the pox] proved invet'rate to.
> Look how they strut it as they go!
> And in the streets make such a show,
> As if they'd there act princes too.
> While th' poet sneaking all alone
> In some by-lane where he's unknown,
> No farther than his pot can go,
> And has a pipe to th' bargain too.

The hirelings had few responsibilities. Most of the younger men rioted away their lives in the taverns and brothels of Covent Garden, Moorfields, and Whetstone's Park, and were always in debt to tradesmen and landladies. Sober Thomas Betterton complained (*in The History of the English Stage,* 1741) that the young men were often given to "undisguised debauchery and drunkenness, coming on the very stage in contempt of the audience when they were scarce able to speak a word." He was disturbed, too, by "the irregularities of the ladies," who were more interested in catching a cully for a husband or a "keeper" than in learning their lines.

The hirelings were poorly paid, rarely earning more than thirty or forty shillings a week (equal in purchasing power to about the same number of dollars today), and they had little hope of advancement. But at least they were the King's, or the Duke's, servants; they could filch fine clothes from the theater's stocks and flaunt them off-stage; they called themselves ladies and gentlemen; they were acceptable at Court, and the men wore swords. Yet the true gentry never recognized players as equals; citizens despised them all as vagabonds and wastrels; and godly people shunned them as arrant devils. Even in the lists of the King's servants the players came last, after the musicians, the huntsmen, and the royal rat-killer.

All the players worked hard for about forty weeks out of the year. The theaters were closed on fast days and during Passion Week in Lent. Because so many of their customers left town in the hot months, the companies fell into the habit of closing for the summer, except for occasional performances put on by the hirelings for their own benefit. The theaters could be closed for four to six weeks because of the death of an adult member of the royal family, temporarily because of a riot or an insult to a powerful lord, and indefinitely because of war or plague. When the theaters were closed, the hirelings starved, and the sharing actors had no dividends.

Usually the actors played six afternoons a week (never on Sundays), rehearsed almost as many mornings, and often put on after-supper performances for the King and Court at Whitehall or for the lawyers and law students at the Inns of Court. Because a new, or newly revived, play seldom lasted for more than three performances, the actors were everlastingly engaged in rehearsals. When a brand-new play was accepted by the company, and the parts had been written out and assigned, the players spent two or three weeks rehearsing it, meanwhile presenting in the afternoons during that period half a dozen or more stock plays from their repertory. Once a part was assigned to a player, he was expected to keep it in memory and to be able to recall it six months or a year later after a sketchy rehearsal. It is hardly surprising that the players were often "out" in their parts.

The first requirement for a good player, therefore, was a retentive memory. The second was physical stamina. Plays moved at a rapid pace, with only brief intervals between acts. In a typical tragedy, the actor fought vigorously with blunted sword and dagger, rallied his troops, made onslaughts and excursions, and bellowed out his passion with a voice that shook the scenes. In a farce the actor was forever climbing ladders, trees, and walls, jumping from windows, hiding under beds and tables, wrestling or fencing with watchmen, wits, and women, and falling through trap doors. Because furniture was rarely used outside the scene area, a player with a major role had few chances to sit down during the three hours' traffic of the stage.

The third requirement was a thorough knowledge of all the behavior patterns appropriate to the Restoration stage. Except for purposes of satiric portraiture — of persons or types — there was no such thing as "natural" acting. No doubt the actors who represented John Dryden as Poet Bayes in Buckingham's *The Rehearsal* (1671), Sir Robert Howard as Sir Positive At-all in Shadwell's *The Sullen Lovers* (1668), and Robert Hooke (curator of the Royal Society) as Sir Nicholas Gimcrack in Shadwell's *The Virtuoso* (1676) strove for realistic, recognizable portraits. Hook went to see *The Virtuoso,* recognized his portrait on the stage, and noted in his diary, "Damned dogs! Vindica me Deus. People almost pointed.") Similarly, when Nell Gwyn in breeches played a typical young gallant in Dryden's *Secret Love* (1667), Mr. Pepys wrote gleefully that she "hath the motions and carriage of a spark the most that ever I saw any man have." Ordinarily the girl in man's clothes made no attempt to conceal her sex behind masculine mannerisms. When the moment of revelation came — when she doffed her periwig, her long hair fell about her ears, and everybody on stage cried, "A woman!" — the audience was not in the least surprised.

For the most part, stage speech and stage conventions followed rigid, long-established conventions. Thus the devices of "asides" and "soliloquies" so frequently found in Restoration plays were inherited from the older stage and made plausible by the continued proximity of actor and audience. An actor spoke a brief aside directly to the audience, while his stage companions looked away and pretended not to hear. In a long soliloquy, the actor, standing alone at the front of the stage, was supposed to be thinking aloud, taking the audience into his confidence, and therefore telling the truth as he saw it.

There was a convention of rapid speech, brisk repartee, and vulgar dialects for comedy and farce, and of singing speech for tragedy. When a tragic actor made love he "canted" or "whined" musically. In a "rant," a long, bravura monologue, he was expected to build slowly to a climax in tone and volume, finishing at the top of his lungs. In dying he was expected to grimace, intone brokenly, and expire on a musical note.

Stage gestures were so conventionalized that the experienced spectator who could not hear well could get at least an inkling of the player's emotion. Thus, to indicate that he had fallen in love an actor stared fixedly at the fair one who caused his pain, folded his arms, and sighed deeply. To show that she returned his passion, the lady reciprocated with "a broken sigh, joined with a fainting look." The posture of a dejected lover was like that of a man hanged, with his hands before him and his head on one side. Sometimes the unhappy lover wandered about the stage sighing, with his hand on his heart and his hat pulled down on his brows.

To indicate reason or thought, the player pointed to his head or tapped his forehead; to register tenderness, pity, or grief, he laid his right hand on his heart. He looked upward to apostrophize the gods, and downward to address Hell. He pointed, beckoned, and waved with his right hand, and held it up, palm vertical like a traffic policeman's, to call a halt or command silence. He shaded his eyes with one hand to peer into the distance, held out both hands, palms up, in token of submission, dropped his hands and bent his head to indicate despair, and held both hands aloft, stepping back a pace, to show amazement. He knelt to plead, stood erect to triumph, shook his fist in anger, beat his breast in sorrow, and flourished a handkerchief to mop up theatrical tears. Heroes moved with a stage strut, heroines swam across the stage or swooned into chairs, villains sneaked, snarled, and gnashed their teeth, and comedians ambled and gamboled.

To the uninitiated such unnatural behavior must have seemed like madness. As the story goes, early one morning three highwaymen riding across the fields near London saw a madman about to commit suicide — or so they thought. He was "walking all alone, making all the gestures imaginable of passion, discontent, and fury, a-casting up his eyes to the sky, displaying his arms abroad, and wringing them together again." Moved by compassion, the thieves secured him and begged him not to kill himself. The madman (Jack Verbruggen, a famous player) cried, "What a plague is all this for? I arn't going to hang, stab, nor drown myself for love. I arn't *in* love. I'm a player only getting my part." Angered by the cheat, the thieves tied the player hand and foot and relieved him of ten shillings and a silver-hilted sword.

The older actors in each theater taught the young people all the conventional gestures and ways of speaking. They taught the young men to fence, and, because comedies often ended in a dance by the entire cast, they taught the young men and women country dances and corantos. They taught good manners: how to behave on the stage as ladies and gentlemen should in real life, and rarely did. They taught the young men how to be brisk and gay with ladies, and the young women how to coquet, to handle a fan, heave their breasts, and make the "doux yeux," or languishing eyes. In his *The Man of Mode* (1676), Etherege presented on the stage a scene which suggests the instructions given to young players. Two characters, Young Bellair and Harriet, are pretending love to deceive their respective parents, who are watching them from one of the doorways. Harriet leans against the far wall, and Bellair, "like a modish spark," amorously entertains her in dumb show.

BELLAIR. (*To Harriet*). Now for a look and gestures that may persuade 'em I am saying all the passionate things imaginable.
HARRIET. Your head a little more on one side. Ease yourself on your left leg and play with your right hand.
BELLAIR. Thus, is it not?
HARRIET. Now set your right leg firm on the ground, adjust your belt, then look about you.
BELLAIR. A little exercising will make me perfect.
HARRIET. Smile, and turn to me again very sparkish.
BELLAIR. Will you take your turn and be instructed?
HARRIET. With all my heart!
BELLAIR. At one motion play your fan, roll your eyes, and then settle a kind look upon me.
HARRIET. So.
BELLAIR. Now spread your fan, look down upon it, and tell the sticks with a finger.
HARRIET. Very modish!
BELLAIR. Clap your hand up to your bosom, hold down your gown, shrug a little, draw up your breasts, and let 'em fall again gently, with a sigh or two.
HARRIET. By the good instructions you give, I suspect you for one of those malicious observers who watch people's eyes, and from innocent looks make scandalous conclusions.
BELLAIR. I know some indeed, who out of mere love to mischief are as vigilant as jealousy itself, and will give you an account of every glance that passes at a play and i' th' Circle.
HARRIET. 'Twill not be amiss now to seem a little pleasant.
BELLAIR. Clap your fan, then, in both your hands, snatch it to your mouth, smile and with a lively motion fling your body

a little forward. So — now spread it; fall back on the sudden, cover your face with it and break out into loud laughter. Take up! look grave and fall a-fanning of yourself. — Admirably well acted!

On a busy morning the theater was a madhouse. On the stage a new play would be in rehearsal. Here a couple of dancers were clogging away; there a singer was learning a new song. In the women's shift the tirewomen were patching and mending, and a young actress was learning to walk gracefully; in the men's shift two young actors were making passes with rapiers; in the scene-room the scenekeepers were hammering; in the pit a playwright was rapidly losing his mind. And over all was the smell of paint, varnish, oranges, burning candles, and unwashed humanity.

Fortunately for the players, the companies accepted anyone who could act, and ignored his private life. Yet everybody in the audience knew about his amours. Some of the actors, and a few of the poets, were as notorious sinners as the weak sisters of the tiring rooms, who could never resist the sweet chink of guineas. Charles Hart was once the lover of the great Duchess of Cleveland, formerly King Charles's mistress. William Wycherley, the poet, was one of her long string of conquests. In 1684 the duchess took Cardell Goodman from the stage, made him her Master of Horse, and lived with him for twelve years. Other actors, known wenchers, were less fortunate, although Jo Haynes once boasted in a prologue that he had been "kept" by a great lady. Some of the actresses were so promiscuous that "as impudent as a big-bellied actress" became a common saying.

In the eighteenth century, Colley Cibber (*Apology*, 1740) pointed out that "The private character of an actor will always more or less affect his public performance. I have seen the most tender sentiment of love in tragedy create laughter, instead of compassion, when it has been applicable to the real engagements of the person that uttered it. I have known good parts thrown up, from an humble consciousness that something in them might put an audience in mind of — what was rather wished might be forgotten. Those remarkable words of Evadne, in *The Maid's Tragedy* — "A maidenhead, Amintor, at my years?" — have sometimes been a much stronger jest for being a true one." Once when Elizabeth Barry, a noted cyprian, was required to say in Tate's *King Lear* that she was armed in her "virgin innocence" the whole house roared with laughter.

Whatever their morals, most of the players were short on education — a university graduate among the men was a rarity — but long on talent. The best players in the two companies were experienced, versatile, and gifted. Such leading men as graceful Charles Hart, "who might teach any king on earth how to comport himself," Thomas Betterton, the greatest theatrical genius of the age, "airy" Henry Harris, Michael Mohun, and William Smith were capable, intelligent men, excellent as the fine gentlemen in comedies or the heroes in tragedies. Betterton kept the stage until well into the eighteenth century. The others passed from the scenes, to be succeeded in turn by new players equally skilled: Cardell Goodman, popularly called "Alexander the Great" because of his success in Lee's *The Rival Queens,* William Mountfort, the perfect "fine gentleman" and an excellent mimic, Joseph Williams, George Powell, and wild, untaught Jack Verbruggen. Similarly Anne and Rebecca Marshall, Mary Lee (alias Lady Slingsby), Elizabeth Barry, and Anne Bracegirdle, "the celebrated virgin," were versatile leading ladies, well endowed with beauty and charm.

Among leading comedians, John Lacy was adept at satirical portraits of Puritans, Presbyterians, Irish bog-trotters, and Scots. Craggy-faced Jo Haynes was at his best as a cheating servant or a low-comedy buffoon; like Lacy he was an excellent solo dancer. Honest Cave Underhill shone as a blockhead or booby, shambling James Nokes as a foolish fop or an old cuckold, plump Anthony Leigh as a lecherous old man, and Thomas Dogget as a "mugging" comedian — "very aspectabund," said John Downes, the prompter (*Roscius Anglicanus,* 1708), "wearing a farce in his face." Elinor Leigh (Tony's wife) was a famous low comedienne, and in high comedy her "line" was superannuated beauties. Vivacious Susannah Mountfort was a versatile comedienne who sparkled in every kind of comic role; to playgoers she was "a miracle."

As in every hard-working repertory company, certain players inevitably became typed because of their physical characteristics, their success in a special "line," or their lack of versatility. Audiences came to expect their appearance in very limited roles. Thus, according to Pepys, Nell Gwyn was delightful in comedy but very bad in tragedy; she herself admitted that she hated "serious parts." In his youth Edward Kynaston was either an epicene beauty or a young lover; in later years he played only parts calling for majesty and stateliness. Katherine Corey, a big woman with a talent for comedy but little beauty, usually played maids, governesses and bawds. Faithful John Richards lacked the ability to play more than valet and footman roles, which he did very well indeed. Elizabeth Boutell, a petite blonde, "generally acted the young, innocent lady whom all the heroes are madly in love with." She had very pretty legs and was popular in "breeches parts" — dressed in boy's clothes.

The best example of the typed actor is Samuel Sandford of the Duke's Company, a crooked little man, obviously designed by nature for villain roles. The audiences had seen him so often in the black wig of villainy that they could not conceive of him as an honest man. But in one play, either by accident or at the actor's request, Sanford played a virtuous role. (Probably the play was Crowne's *Regulus* (1692), in which he played Hamilcar, "A noble Carthaginian, Prince of the Senate.") According to Colley Cibber, "The pit, after they had sat three or four acts in a quiet expectation that the well-dissembled honesty of Sandford (for such of course they concluded it) would soon be discovered, or at least, from its security, involve the actors in the play in some surprising distress or confusion, when, at last, finding no such matter, but that the catastrophe had taken quite another turn, and that Sandford was really an honest man to the end of the play, they fairly damned it, as if the author had imposed upon them the most frontless or incredible absurdity." No wonder the pit felt cheated; it wanted to see Sandford tortured and executed. Richard Steele remembered, "When poor Sandford was upon the stage, I have seen him groaning upon a wheel, stuck with daggers, impaled alive, calling his executioners with a dying voice, cruel dogs, and villains! And all this to please his judicious spectators, who were wonderfully delighted with seeing a man in torment so well acted." Sandford may not have been a great actor, but he was a magnificent villain.

Restoration drama was interpreted by players whose skills ran the gamut from mediocrity to greatness. We can imagine how the run-of-stage player performed a role, but the art of the truly great actor is as hard to grasp as a moonbeam and as transitory as a May-fly. The grace of action exists only for the moment and lingers in memory no longer than an after-image on the retina. With the best will in the world, the writer who has seen a great player at his best can give us only a pale impression of his art, which depends on a multitude of small gestures, expressions, and vocal inflections. And no one can describe or explain the mysterious personal magnetism by which the great artist draws his auditors to him and holds them all in the hollow of his hand.

Colley Cibber, a witness of Betterton's acting at its height, tried to describe the great actor's art and gave up. "The most that a Vandyke can arrive at is to make his portraits of great persons seem to *think;* a Shakespeare goes farther yet and tells you *what* his pictures thought; a Betterton steps beyond 'em all, and calls them from the grave to breathe and be themselves again in feature, speech, and motion. When the skillful actor shows you all these powers at once united, and gratifies at once your eye, your ear, your understanding — to conceive the pleasure rising from such harmony, you must have been present at it! 'tis not to be told you!"

*** 4 ***

The Audience

IN GOOD KING CHARLES's not-so-golden days (1660–1685) the theaters were dominated by a Court-and-Town coterie. The Courtiers were the lords, ladies, knights, dames, and lesser gentry who, as the King's or the Duke of York's servants, lodged in the sprawling congeries of chambers at Whitehall or St. James's Palace. The Town included all the wealthy, fashionable folk, habitués of the Court, who had mansions or lodgings in Piccadilly, St. James's Square, along the Strand, or in Covent Garden. A fringe group surrounding this aristocratic society was made up of politicians, place-holders, minor officials (like Mr. Pepys), clerks in government offices, officers in the army or navy, country gentlemen and their wives seeing the sights of London, Members of Parliament, university students on vacation, law students from the Inns of Court, footmen and maids in the upper galleries, and the inevitable *bona robas,* or vizard masks (otherwise fireships, punks, or whores), soliciting custom. In the pit of a theater, foppish young men who loved to display their finery while combing their flaxen periwigs occupied "Fop Corner" near the stage. Gentlemen who fancied themselves as critics — the bane of all dramatists — herded together in the center to pass judgment audibly on a play. More sedate gentry sat with their wives or mistresses in the side-boxes. The King's and the Duke of York's boxes were at the rear of the pit, facing the stage. When they were not occupied by royalty, the boxes were rented at the standard price — four shillings a seat.

Now and then some citizens (from "the City," the mercantile section of London) appeared in the middle or upper galleries — occasionally the Duke's Theater, which was near the City, had a swarm of apprentices in the pit — but in general the sober middle classes avoided the theaters at this time as dens of iniquity and vice. Of course clergymen and nonconformist "fanatics" gave them a wide berth. As Mr. Testimony, in Crowne's *Sir Courtly Nice*, protested, "I was only deluded the other day to a playhouse, and truly it will be a burden to my spirit whilst I live." The chances are that the nonjuring clergyman Jeremy Collier (who refused to take an oath of allegiance to William and Mary), author of *The Immorality and Profaneness of the English Stage* (1698), was never in his life inside a theater.

The coterie was a closed circle of aristocrats, united against the common herd. It was so small that by the time a new play had been on the boards for three or four days, everyone had seen it. Frequently a crowded pit in one theater meant an almost empty house for the other. The coterie used the theaters as private clubhouses, places to which one went to see and be seen, to while away an idle hour or two, to make an assignation or to meet a mistress, to chat with friends and hear all the latest news and gossip. Sometimes a gentleman dropped in at one theater, watched an act, and then ambled to the other playhouse for a brief visit — paying nothing at either house.

Soon after their midday dinner (the heaviest meal of the day), people began drifting into the pit and boxes. Often they wandered about over the benches or among the boxes while a play was in progress, and talked right through the performance, annoying such theater buffs as Mr. Pepys. They basked in the glory of the King's (or the Duke of York's) presence, and paid polite deference to their betters. Once Mr. Pepys commented,

"But it was pleasant to see how everybody rose up when my Lord John Butler, the Duke of Ormonde's son, came into the pit toward the end of the play." A duke's son was a very important person.

The coterie came to the theater to be entertained, not to be edified or reformed. Its tastes in drama were essentially conservative; it liked novelty, but not too much novelty. Its tastes could be changed, but only slowly, and only when old themes had become hackneyed by repetition. It wanted to see itself pictured on the stage, not as it really was, but as it liked to think of itself — as the finest product of modern civilization, brilliant, witty, cultured, and refined. It was self-conscious and class-conscious.

Restoration society was a pyramid, with the King and the royal family at its pinnacle. Below in the pecking order came the nobility: dukes (with the King's bastards first), marquises, earls, viscounts, and barons. Bishops and archbishops ranked as lords and sat in the House of Lords. Next came a broad band of gentry: baronets (whose titles could be inherited), knights, doctors, lawyers, clergymen, and all those qualified (or impudent enough) to write "Esquire" after their names. The solid bulk of the pyramid was made up of countrymen and citizens — yeomen, tenant farmers, merchants, craftsmen, apprentices, and laborers — who, in the eyes of the coterie, were useful animals of no social or political consequence. The aristocrats laughed at the lower classes, sneered at them, and detested them, partly to affirm their own superiority, partly because in the days of Oliver Cromwell the rude mechanicals had pillaged, oppressed, exiled, and imprisoned gentlemen of birth and breeding. Even Mr. Pepys (the son of a tailor!) could hardly bear the sight of citizens in a theater.

King Charles was by far the most important member of the coterie. He went to the theaters often, taking with him a retinue of Court functionaries and Court ladies. Without his patronage the playhouses would have suffered seriously. When his dark, saturnine face cracked into a laugh, the audience laughed with him. His presence could make a new play successful; if he came to its first day (when double prices were charged), the players were assured of a full house. His verdict could make or mar a playwright or a player. He encouraged the dramatic poets, suggesting to them themes and plots. Always receptive to the players, his servants, he listened to their troubles, settled their quarrels, and did his best to protect them from bullies, ruffians, and rioters. When they played at his private theater in Whitehall, he saw to it that they were plentifully supplied with meat, bread, beer, sack, and claret. Easy King Charles was a very popular monarch.

Most of the ladies in a typical audience were intelligent and well educated; that is, they could keep accounts and read and write, although their spelling was wonderful to behold. They could speak French, play a musical instrument, sing, dance, embroider, sew, and make jellies and conserves. What more could a husband desire? The ladies' taste in drama was for romance and scenes of tender, idealized love. Most of the gentlemen had some learning, and many were products of Oxford, Cambridge, or the Inns of Court; they were intelligent men with a wide spectrum of interests, but they were not thinkers. Their knowledge of the Latin poets and historians was fairly extensive; some were well read in moral philosophy and in English, French, Spanish, or Italian literature; and some were judicious critics of the arts. They liked plays with intellectual substance. The older men had seen upon the Caroline stage the plays of Shakespeare, Jonson, Beaumont and Fletcher, and the lesser Elizabethans, and had decided views about the nature and quality of good drama. But few knew anything at all about geography, mathematics, or the natural sciences; and some barbarians knew nothing at all about anything.

Most of the Court and Town were ostensibly religious — members of the Anglican Church in good standing — and surprisingly superstitious for an "enlightened" age. Storms, comets, eclipses, and heavenly fires were portents of disaster, of God's wrath to be visited upon the sinful earth. Some of the gentry believed in witches, ghosts, and devils, and feared a literal hell. Most of them still believed in alchemy and horoscopy; the Duke of Buckingham spent a fortune in alchemical experiments, and John Dryden cast horoscopes for himself and his family. The members of the coterie were caught between the credulity of the past and the new scientific skepticism represented by the Royal Society. They had heard about the theories of Copernicus, Galileo, Harvey, Bacon, and Descartes, but they only half accepted them; they had been brought up to believe that the Bible was the great book of scientific truth; and where the Bible was silent, Galen and Aristotle spoke with authority. Yet they found the appeal to reason as against authority immensely attractive. They had been taught that man, having freedom of moral choice, must pay the piper if he chose to dance along the primrose path. At the same time, painful experience — especially during the Interregnum — had led them to cynicism, to the belief that human conduct was motivated by self-interest only, and that justice, while very pretty on the stage, was to be found neither here nor hereafter. They liked to see self-interest versus altruism debated on the stage, but they knew the answers in advance.

A small but important band of Court intellectuals, influenced by the materialism of Hobbes's *Leviathan,* were downright skeptics or empiricists who feared neither heaven nor hell and lived for the rational gratification of their senses. As hedonists their motto was, in effect, "carpe diem" — enjoy the day. To godly people they were truly "the sons of Belial, flown with insolence and wine." To the Court and Town they were delightfully wicked gentry, the leaders of taste and literary fashion, and ideal models for the comedy of wit.

Initially the members of a typical Restoration audience were cavaliers, strong royalists, reacting violently against the republican commonwealth which had ended in 1660. After the so-called Popish Plot of 1678, when the royalists became known as Tories and the new republicans (followers of Lord Shaftesbury) as Whigs, the Tories continued to control the theaters, and, until the Whig triumph of 1689, Whig poets had difficulty getting their plays produced. The Tories were not absolutists, but they firmly believed in the inherent rights of kings. Extremists believed in "Divine Right"; to them the King was sacred as head of the established church ("Defender of the Faith") and God's vicegerent on earth. Those who worked to change the frame of things were sinful rebels. Of course, there were cynics who, while professing loyalty, sought to sell their services to the King and his ministers. A few ambitious politicians even sacrificed their wives' or their daughters' virtue to get pelf, places, and preferment. The skeptical Earl of Rochester once wrote to his friend, Henry Savile, "They who would be great in our little government seem as ridiculous to me as schoolboys, who with much endeavor and some danger climb a crab tree, venturing their necks for fruit which solid pigs would disdain if they were not starving." Nevertheless, kingship was still considered the summit of earthly felicity, in reality and on the stage, and second only to kingship was a footstool near the throne.

Gentry of almost any age from sixteen to sixty went to the theaters. By the time they reached their majority, most young gentlemen were married, and many were already fathers. But since marriages in aristocratic circles were usually arranged by parents or guardians on the basis of suitability of age, fortune, rank, and reputation (a bride must be virtuous), the young husbands rarely troubled their heads about their wives. Some young couples were so compatible that they fell in love after marriage and lived together in domestic bliss. Most young husbands fulfilled their conjugal duties faithfully (one must have children to inherit an estate and carry on a name) and were formally attentive to their wives in public, but for their pleasure they kept mistresses or patronized the brothels of "Lady" Bennett, "Mother" Moseley, or "Madam" Temple, to name only a few famous bawds. Courtiers who left their wives in the country to look after their estates and children often flaunted their mistresses openly in the theaters, following the example of King Charles, with his rout of titled and untitled doxies. The fact that most aristocratic marriages were arranged debased the institution to the level of a commercial alliance and made a mockery of the sacrament.

Restoration gentlemen were well-bred, but some of their manners would shame a tramp. They were polite to others of their own class; they bowed, embraced each other, and "saluted" ladies with ceremonial kisses, but their speech was coarse, profane, and pungent with four-letter Anglo-Saxon words, even before ladies. They ate with knives and fingers, drank to excess, used the fireplaces as privies, spat on the floors, and rarely bathed. The ladies were little better. In Wycherley's *The Plain Dealer* (1676), Olivia spat on the floor at every mention of "filthy china." Once in the theater a lady spat backward on Mr. Pepys. Observing that she did not know he was there and that she was very pretty, he said nothing.

The gentry had refined tastes in art and enjoyed balls, masques, and music meetings, but they shared also in the brutal amusements of the uncouth mob. Gentlemen and their families thronged to Tyburn, Charing Cross, and Tower Hill to witness executions. Perhaps they flinched when the axe thudded home, and the bloody head rolled in the dust; or when Jack Ketch, the hangman, pushed a condemned felon from his ladder, cut him down, cut off his privy parts, ripped him open, cast his entrails on a fire, and chopped his body into pieces to be empaled on the City gates; or when a woman who had murdered her husband or clipped the King's coins (both crimes were listed as petty treason) was burned alive at Tyburn. If the gentry turned their heads away from such horrid sights they have left no record of their squeamishness. Mr. Pepys made a special trip to Charing Cross to see one of the regicides, Major-General Harrison, hanged, "which was done there, he looking as cheerful as any man could in that condition. He was presently cut down and his head and heart shown to the people, at which there were great shouts of joy." To compete with such exhibitions, the playwrights had to invent even bloodier and more sensational scenes for the stage.

Lacking the delights of an execution, one could find cock-fighting, dog-fighting, bull-baiting and bear-baiting at the Beargarden in Southwark across the river. For such events the theaters could offer no competition. Bull-baiting, reported John Evelyn, was a "rude and dirty pastime." He was present one day when "one of the bulls tossed a dog full into a lady's lap as she sat in one of the boxes at a considerable height from the arena." Then there was sword-fighting at the Beargarden or in Gibbons' Tennis Court (after the King's Company left it), where men fought until they were covered with blood, and the screaming rabble flung pennies on the stage. Bartholomew and Southwark fairs provided such coarse amusements as rope-dancers, mountebanks, and "Jack Pudding" clowns; prize-fighters, who fought with swords and cudgels; low-comedy drolls; puppet shows; and such strange sights as an elephant, a rhinoceros, a crocodile, or a giantess. Like most of his subjects, good King Charles had vulgar tastes. He enjoyed cock-fighting at Newmarket as much as he enjoyed horse-racing, the sport of kings, and he relished also the rope-dancing of Jacob Hall in the Banqueting House at Whitehall. Early in his reign there were wrestling matches and annual bear-baitings in the Tiltyard at Whitehall. In 1673 both bulls and bears were baited at Whitehall, and in 1679 the King entertained the Spanish Ambassador with a great bear-baiting in the Beargarden.

Every gentleman wore a sword as a part of his daily costume; he was a skilled fencer, and a keen critic of sword-play on the stage. He was touchy about his public image, his "honor," and quick to flare up at a real or fancied insult. To protect his reputation and good name, he was willing to risk his life in a duel. Mimic duels were almost daily routine on the stage, and real sword fights in the theaters while a play was in progress, or set duels elsewhere resulting from quarrels in the theaters, were not uncommon.

In 1667, for example, a quarrel in a playhouse between the Duke of Buckingham and Henry Killigrew was very nearly fatal to Killigrew. In 1673 a general melee near the door of the Theater Royal resulted in wounds to Lord Buckhurst, Capt.

Bulkeley, and Col. Strode. In August, 1675, "Mr. Scrope, sitting by Sir Thomas Armstrong at the Duke's playhouse, struck him on the shins twice; both men wished to speak to Mrs. Uphill, a [King's Company] player who came into the house masked. The gentlemen round made a ring, and they fought. Sir Thomas killed Scrope at the first pass." Three months later, in the same theater, the mad Earl of Pembroke fought with Mr. Charles Davenant. Both were wounded. In 1679 John Churchill (the future great Duke of Marlborough) beat "an orange wench in the Duke's playhouse," and was challenged by Thomas Otway, the poet. On the field of honor, "both were wounded, but Churchill most." In 1682 "Mr. Vaughan and Mr. Charles Deering fought . . . and the last dangerously hurt — on the playhouse stage." According to another account, the duellists leaped on the stage, brushed the players aside, and went to it. In 1684 "Sir James Hackett . . . was wounded in the thigh by one Mr. Potter in the playhouse, of which wound he has since died." A year later the bellicose Mr. Charles Deering killed a Capt. Goring in a duel in one of the tiring rooms of a theater. Both men were drunk. In 1695 Mr. Young and Mr. Carew, who had quarreled about a woman in the playhouse the night before, killed each other in a set duel in Hyde Park. Later that year, the newswriters reported, "Two of our sparks coming out of the playhouse in Dorset Gardens fell out about a miss of the town and one of them is killed, the other committed to Newgate." In April, 1700, "Mr. William Squibb, a clerk of the Exchequer, was severely wounded by Capt. Francis in the playhouse; the quarrel was said to be about pulling off a gentlewoman's mask in the pit."

Of course there were laws against dueling, and frequent royal proclamations against the practice were published, but no gentleman needed to fear punishment unless his victim had powerful friends. The fact that he had killed in defense of his honor was considered a valid excuse. At worst he could be convicted of manslaughter, plead benefit of clergy, and be burnt in the hand — with a cold iron.

It is not surprising that, in an epilogue intended for *The Duke of Guise* (1682), Dryden begged the "bilbo gallants" in the audience to keep the peace or to take their duels elsewhere:

> If not, I swear we'll pull up all our benches,
> Not for your sakes, but for our orange-wenches;
> For you thrust wide sometimes, and many a spark
> That misses one, can hit the other mark.
> This makes our boxes full, for men of sense
> Pay their four shillings in their own defense,
> That safe behind the ladies they may stay,
> Peep o'er the fan, and judge the bloody fray.

A rough audience has no patience with the nice refinements of genteel drama, and in the later years of King Charles the coterie was dominated by its rougher members. The prologues and epilogues of Restoration plays are filled with complaints about the noise, rudeness, and brawls in the audience, complaints which increase in number and sharpness as the years march on. Although Mr. Pepys (between 1660 and 1669) was occasionally annoyed by talkers in the pit, he recorded no brawls or disturbances. But by the 1670s theatrical manners were rapidly declining. The older group of playgoers, bred up in the theatrical decorum of pre-commonwealth days, was dwindling away, and a new generation of wild young blades and bullies was invading the theaters. As Shadwell wrote in his epilogue to Maidwell's *The Loving Enemies* (1680),

> Oh! How severe is our poor poet's fate,
> Who in this barren trade begins so late!
> True wit's no longer current, 'tis cried down,
> And all your half-wits into knavery grown.
> Those who once loved the stage are now in years,
> And leave good poets for dull pamphleteers,
> Nay, for the worst of rascals, libeleers.
> In none of these will the young sparks delight,
> They never read, and scorn all those that write.

They only come the boxes to survey,
Laugh, roar and bawl, but never hear the play;
In monkey's tricks they pass the time away.

Young men in pairs and packs came bawling into the pit, usually flushed with wine. They swore, talked bawdy at the tops of their voices, quarreled with the orange wenches and each other, and gathered chattering about a vizard mask, commenting on her looks, her age, and her probable diseases. They "dumbfounded" an innocent spectator — striking him from behind and looking demure when he turned. They twirled hats, pulled periwigs, jostled the benches, and threw fruit. They commented audibly on the play, guffawed at serious speeches and hissed at comedies. Dramatists pilloried them on the stage, and prologue writers railed against the "damned pirates of the pit" and the "doughty bullies" who caterwauled in the middle galleries while their lackeys roared like bears in the upper galleries. No one heeded their protests, and the players could do nothing to suppress the brutes. They were gentlemen.

The original coterie of sophisticated aristocrats was rapidly disintegrating when, in February, 1685, King Charles II died, and his brother came to the throne as James II. In the short, troubled reign of James, the coterie finally disappeared, destroyed by James's bigoted policy of replacing all Protestant courtiers with ardent Catholics, and discouraging the Protestant loyalists of the Town, most of whom retired to their country estates. In 1689, when the Whigs triumphed at last, and William and Mary entered on their joint reign, the typical audience was no longer a unified blend of Court and Town, and, because King William cared nothing for the theater, it had no leader. New components entered, chiefly the *nouveaux riches* of the City. The fops, beaux, and bullies crowded not only the pit but the stage itself, and disorders increased as faction warred with faction. One who had a personal or political grudge against a playwright or a player could assemble his friends in the theater and with whistles, hisses, and catcalls ruin a play. "I'll tell you their method," said Philabel in Granvile's *The She-Gallants* (1695); "they spread themselves in parties all over the house, some in the pit, some in the boxes, others in the galleries, but principally on the stage. They cough, sneeze, talk loud, and break silly jests; sometimes laughing, sometimes singing, sometimes whistling, till the house is in an uproar. Some laugh and clap; some hiss and are angry; swords are drawn, the actors interrupted, the scene broken off, and so the play's sent to the devil."

The social and intellectual decadence of the audience brought on a decadence of drama, which, with some notable exceptions, broke down into bawdy farces, foolish operas, sensational melodramas, and pathetic tragedies. Sentimentalism came in at the door, the tragic spirit flew out the window, and the comic spirit dissolved in tears.

*** 5 ***

The Poets

EARLY IN 1672 Mr. Elkanah Settle finished a heroic play which seemed to him very good indeed. As he told the story in his *A Narrative* (1683), "I carried it to His Majesty's Theater, where in the height of Mr. Hart's health and excellence, I flattered myself with assurance of wonderful success from the performance of so able a company." The King's Comany accepted the play gladly, and even had Settle sworn in as "sewer in ordinary to His Majesty, being one of the poets in His Majesty's Theater Royal." But Settle had forgotten, or chose to ignore, "former treaties with His Highness' servants." The Duke's Company, which had produced his first play, *Cambyses* (1671), had an option on his second effort. Learning what was going on, the Duke's Company complained to the Duke of York, a very partial judge, who, not unexpectedly, decided that his own players had first rights to the play. From his verdict there was no appeal.

On the whole, although Settle probably had to do some rewriting to adapt his play to another company, he was lucky. The King's Company, forced by its fire on January 26, 1672, to work in the cramped spaces of Lisle's Tennis Court, could have done very little with his opus. Instead, a group of amateurs, "persons of such birth and honor that they borrowed no greatness from the characters they acted," produced *The Empress of Morocco* at Court in the spring of 1673; the Duke's Company gave it a magnificent public production in June of that year, and Settle's bookseller, William Cademan, brought it out with six elegant, full-page engravings of scenes from the play, which made printing history. But Settle was a stubborn fellow. He nursed his "malignant resentment" against the Duke of York for seven long years and even wrote a pamphlet against him, *The Character of a Popish Successor* (1681). In *A Narrative* he recanted his Whiggish heresy and begged the Duke's pardon.

The lot of a professional playwright in Restoration England was not a happy one. When he had two theaters to choose from, he had to write his play with an eye to the actors in one company; if that troupe refused it, he might have to re-write it for the other players. Because the companies were notably reluctant to pay for new scenes and new clothes, he had to bear in mind the stock scenes and the costumes of each theater. He had to use as many of the salaried hirelings as he could, and to create roles suited to the special talents of popular players. Sometimes he went so far as to discuss a role with a player before writing it. When there was only one company (from 1682 to 1695), he had to compete with a vast number of stock plays, which the thrifty actors, blessed with a monopoly, chose to revive instead of presenting costly new plays.

If a company of players decided to produce his opus, the poet spent several hours with them, reading the play aloud with grace notes and flourishes. He spent many mornings in the theater while the play was in rehearsal. To get the best out of the players, he had to flatter them, give them little presents, and, whenever possible, "fatten" their parts. Well aware that a first-rate prologue or epilogue could make a mediocre play successful, he racked his brains for clever variations on shopworn themes, or paid John Dryden two or three guineas for a sheaf of witty couplets.

At last came the first day, usually toward the end of the week, when more people had the leisure to go to a theater. Behind the scenes stood the poet in suffering suspense, listening for laughter and applause. Would the play last for three performances? If it did, he would get the net profits of the third performance, "the poet's day," some £50 or so, plus whatever he could squeeze out of a bookseller for the copyright of the play. No doubt some poets got more. It is said, for example, that Otway got £100 apiece for his *The Orphan* (1680) and *Venice Preserved* (1682); that Shadwell gained £130 from the third day of *The Squire of Alsatia* (1688); and that in addition to his earnings of £140 for *The Fatal Marriage* (1694) fifty noblemen gave Southerne a guinea apiece, and the bookseller paid £36 for the right to print the play. One suspects some exaggeration. If the play failed to run for at least three days, the poet got nothing. At least, by virtue of having had a play produced, he was ever after admitted free into the pit.

If a play was very successful, the company might offer the playwright a contract for his next effort and a small weekly retaining fee (a "pension") to keep him from starving while he wrote another play. Most professional writers were tied to a company by some such agreement, or were shareholders. John Dryden, for example, "binding himself to write 3 plays a year, was admitted and continued as a sharer in the King's Playhouse for divers years, and received for his share and a quarter 3 or 4 hundred pounds" a year. (Obviously he must have given up the profits for his third days.) In ten years Dryden wrote only nine plays for the King's Company, but the actors were not dissatisfied until he himself broke the agreement by peddling to the rival company a play he had written in collaboration with Nathaniel Lee, *Oedipus* (1678).

The professional poet had to compete not only with his fellows but with a host of genteel amateurs — in Pope's phrase, "the mob of gentlemen who wrote with ease." At the Court of King Charles II, a gentleman who could tune a love song or scribble a play was on the high road to royal favor. It is a moot question whether he wrote for fame or preferment; but it is certainly true that a witty courtier with a gift for verse or drama could become one of the King's band of pensioners, a Gentleman of the Privy Chamber, an envoy to a foreign prince, or a commissioner for hackney coaches with a salary and fat fees. Most amateurs were content to write only one play; some wrote two or three, or tinkered with older plays. Among the amateurs were two dukes, four earls, a viscount, a baron, fifteen knights and baronets, and dozens of esquires. Now and then a truly modest "person of quality" contributed an anonymous play. The fact that the literary lordlings scorned the rewards of a third day (sometimes they gave them to a protégée) tended to keep down the rates of pay for the professionals.

There was some compensation in the fact that upper-class interest in dramatic literature led to widespread patronage. For a fulsome dedication prefixed to a printed play, a dramatist could expect to get a substantial reward from his noble patron — at least ten guineas. Patrons contributed prologues, epilogues, and songs to plays written by their professional friends, often entertained their pet poets at dinner, and sometimes gave them food and lodging in palatial country houses while they wrote their plays.

The professional writer had to please the coterie of nobles and gentles in the audience, the fops and beaux, the country squires, the law students, the politicians, clerks, and bullies. The box-office, of course, is the first problem of a playwright in any age — "the drama's laws the drama's patrons give." The Restoration writer had to bear in mind the politics, tastes, and prejudices of his present or potential patrons, and he had to keep a wary eye out for the Lord Chamberlain of the Household. That functionary, or his deputy, the Master of the Revels, had full power to censor plays, to cut out passages offensive to official ears, and, if he chose, to forbid production. Political plays had to reflect the views of the establishment. Because the murder of a mimic king in a tragedy — even a wicked king — might give someone dangerous ideas, no stage monarch could be killed by a "good" character. Divinity hedged a king in make-believe. Satire, except when it was directed against the coterie's enemies, or against unworthy upstarts who were not to the manner born, was risky. There was always the chance that some powerful lord, fancying himself libeled, might get the play stopped. Thus Dryden's *The Kind Keeper, or Mr. Limberham* (1678), a satire against the "crying sin of keeping," was suppressed after its third day by a clutch of lordly lechers who took offense. In *A Satyr against Keeping,* Cleve, a very minor poet, wrote,

> Dryden, good man, thought keepers to reclaim,
> Wrote a kind satire, called it *Limberham.*
> This all the herd of lechers straight alarms,
> From Charing Cross to Bow are up in arms;
> They damned the play all at one fatal blow,
> And broke the glass that did their pictures show.

The professional poets suffered also from the envious attacks of rival writers, from the sneers of such arrogant noblemen as Lord Rochester (who once said of Dryden, "He is a rarity which I cannot but be fond of, as one would be of a hog that could fiddle, or a singing owl"), and from the strictures of such pretentious critics as Langbaine, Rymer, Dennis, and Blackmore. Prologues and epilogues against the ignorance, malice, and caprice of critics (especially against the captious amateurs in the pit) increase steadily throughout the period. The critics could damn a play for irregularity, bombast, bawdry, or downright dullness, but their worst charge against a poet was plagiarism. The Elizabethans could borrow at will from the storehouse of European fiction and drama, but the Restoration poet did so at his peril. Unconcerned about how artistically he used his borrowed material, the critics condemned him for plagiarism, which they considered shameless theft. Gerard Langbaine's *An Account of the English Dramatic Poets* (1691) is largely a catalogue of plagiarisms. Langbaine beat over a wide field of foreign and domestic narratives, past and present, hunting sources for the plots of modern plays, and whenever he flushed one, even out of a remote, unlikely thicket, he pointed and barked, quivering with excitement.

When the poets failed to follow the rigid rules set up by neoclassic critics, they had to endure cold abuse. Neoclassicism was based on the assumption that no one could write a poem or a play which would be better than those of Homer, Virgil, Horace, and the Greek and Roman dramatists. Drawing their precepts from the practices of classic writers, modified and enlarged by the successive rules of Aristotle, Scaliger, and Boileau, the neoclassic critics insisted that modern writers should imitate the austerity, regularity, decorum, and elegance of their remote predecessors. The "rules" were as strict as the Commandments; as Pope wrote in his *Essay on Criticism* (1711),

> Those rules of old discovered, not devised,
> Are Nature still, but Nature methodized;
> Nature, like liberty, is but restrained
> By the same laws which first herself ordained. . . .
> Learn hence for ancient rules a just esteem;
> To copy Nature is to copy them.

The neoclassicists insisted particularly on the observance of the dramatic unities. A play should have unity of action — only one plot. It should have unity of place — the setting should be limited to the confines of a single city, and ideally to a single house or room. It should have unity of time — the period supposedly covered by the events of a play should never be more than twenty-four hours, and ideally it should be no more than the real time of action on the stage. The neoclassicists insisted also on decorum. Kings and queens should speak and act like royal persons, and peasants like peasants. Tragic heroes should speak in verse, and comic characters in prose. Violence, torture, and murder should take place off-stage, and the events should be reported by messengers. "You must not bring upon the stage," said Horace, "things fit only to be acted behind the scenes." Because the average playgoer thumbed his nose at neoclassicism, and the poets, perforce, gave him the variety, excitement, and blood he demanded, the poor poets were forever suffering from the slings and arrows of outraged critics.

The Elizabethan dramatist, writing in an expansive age of exuberant activity and exciting discovery, had a world of subjects to choose from. The Restoration serious dramatist, hedged about by restrictions on all sides, was limited to a narrow range of subjects: chiefly love, ambition, revenge, villainy, and war; and the comic dramatist was limited to intrigue, farce, fornication, and folly. The aristocratic audience had not the slightest interest in realistic treatments of political or social injustice, corruption and immorality in government, the grinding poverty of the lower classes, or the problems of farmers, merchants, craftsmen, and Quakers. The Restoration dramatist had to remember that, whether he wrote in verse or in what Dryden called "that other harmony of prose," he was a poet — one whose work was expected to appeal to the imagination and give pleasure. He was an entertainer, not a philosopher, a social commentator, or a moralist. Let him preach morality as much as he liked, so long as it was upper-class morality. Let him present characters from every walk of life, but let it be understood that truly fashionable folk must be admirable, and that shoemakers, porters, shopkeepers, bawds, bumpkins, fanatics, and upstarts must be made as ridiculous as possible.

Above all, the members of a typical audience valued wit; they cared less for what was said than for how it was said. In the seventeenth century "wit" had many meanings. Among the beaux and bullies a wit was a practical joker in the theater, adept at "dumbfounding" and at "selling bargains" to victims — talking a lot of grave nonsense which led at last to a whoop of "Whip-stitch, kiss my arse," while all the bullies doubled up with laughter. In the streets, the bullies ("scowrers" or "hectors") were at their wittiest, breaking windows, beating pedestrians, and assaulting the watch. Wycherley's Novel, in *The Plain Dealer,* insisted that there was both wit and humor in breaking windows.

OLDFOX. Pure rogue! there's your modern wit for you! wit and humor in breaking of windows! There's mischief, if you will, but no wit or humor.

NOVEL. Prithee, prithee, peace, old fool. I tell you, where there's mischief, there's wit. Don't we admit the monkey a wit among beasts, only because he's mischievous? And let me tell you, as good nature is a sign of a fool, being mischievous is a sign of a wit.

At Court a wit was a raconteur or conversationalist, clever at repartee and *double entendre,* critical and often malicious, who occasionally said something memorable. In this sense, King Charles was a wit. On a still higher level, a wit was an intellectual, a philosopher or learned man, who spooned out his wisdom in pithy sayings and epigrams. Or a wit was a poet. Every dramatist yearned to be known as a wit, to be famed for his fancy and judgment.

Dryden defined literary wit (as apart from comic wit) first by its negatives. It was not, he said, a thin conceit, the ghost of a jest, the mere sting of an epigram, the seeming contradiction of a poor antithesis, or the morality of a sentential speech. "*Wit writing,*" he said, "is no other than the faculty of imagination in the writer, which, like a nimble spaniel, beats over and ranges through the field of memory, till it springs the quarry it hunted after. *Wit written* is that which is well defined, the happy result of thought, or product of imagination." And, finally, wit "is a propriety of thoughts and words; or, in other terms, thoughts and words elegantly adapted to the subject." Pope oversimplified this concept when he wrote,

True wit is Nature to advantage dressed,
What oft was thought, but ne'er so well expressed.

Addison pointed out, rightly, that Dryden's conclusion "is not so properly a definition of wit, as of good writing in general." In modern terms, if literature may be defined as the interpretation of experience by an artist, literary wit would be the total skill of the artist — his imaginative ingenuity, his understanding, his ability to organize his thoughts, and his verbal felicity.

Oddly enough, wits famed for their conversation rarely succeeded as playwrights. When Sir Charles Sedley, reputed a great wit, wrote a comedy called *The Mulberry Garden* (1668), Mr. Pepys reported that "all the world do expect great matters." All the world was disappointed; "though there was, here and there, a pretty saying, and that not very many neither, yet the whole play had nothing extraordinary in it, neither of language nor design." The Duke of Buckingham was famous as a wit, farceur, and buffoon, yet his burlesque, *The Rehearsal* (1671), required the collaborative efforts of three wits, Thomas Sprat, Samuel Butler, and Martin Clifford, and was years in the making.

To be a successful playwright, one had to study the stage, the actors, and the audience, to learn the rhetorical structure of good dramatic speech and the dramatic structure of a good play — and all the technical tricks by which a poet could move his audience to laughter or tears. One had to watch closely the audience's reactions to stock characters and familiar themes, and to read widely in drama and dramatic criticism. Often an experienced but unlearned actor could write a better play than the most profound scholar or the most brilliant Court wit. John Lacy, William Mountfort, George Powell, and Colley Cibber, all successful actors, were also successful playwrights. John Dryden, Thomas Shadwell, Aphra Behn, John Crowne, Thomas D'Urfey, Nathaniel Lee, Elkanah Settle, Thomas Otway, and Edward Ravenscroft — professionals who produced more than a hundred and fifty successful plays between 1660 and 1700 — were earnest students of the drama and stage, constantly at work in their laboratory, the theater. Let us exonerate them of any urge to elevate the stage or — in spite of their repeated protestations — to reform the age. They worked to earn their livings. None of them got rich.

*** 6 ***

The Tragic Buskin

TRUE TRAGEDY brings chaos into an ordered world; comedy brings only confusion. When tragedy strikes a human life, it brings black chaos which can never again take form; but the confusion of comedy is easily cleared up and no harm is done. Tragedy tends to flourish in an age of faith and high aspiration; comedy in an age of skepticism and indifference. Tragedy evokes terror and tears; comedy provides reassurance and laughter.

Although more comedies than tragedies were written for the Restoration stage (roughly a three to two ratio), tragedy was traditionally considered the higher art, and the craft of the stage tragedian was honored above that of the comedian. Almost every professional poet tried his hand at some variety of serious play, which he usually called a tragedy.

The label is misleading. In the seventeenth century "tragedy" was a wide net which enclosed every kind of serious play, including what Dryden once sneered at as "that inferior sort of tragedies which end with a prosperous event" — a happy ending. Even an opera could be called a tragedy. Sometimes a romantic play with a happy ending was labeled a tragicomedy, in accordance with John Fletcher's definition: "Tragicomedy is not so called in respect of mirth and killing, but in respect it wants death, which is enough to make it no tragedy, yet brings some near it, which is enough to make it no comedy." (We would call such a play a melodrama.) In this sense, Stapylton's *The Step-Mother* (1663) is properly entitled "A Tragi-Comedy," yet Digby's near-tragic *Elvira* (1664) is called "A Comedy." More often a tragicomedy was a play with two plots, one serious and one comic, loosely linked together. But Dryden's *Marriage à la Mode* (1672), which fits this definition, is labeled "A Comedy," and Southerne's *The Fatal Marriage* (1694), which consists of a comedy and a pathetic tragedy tacked together, is described as "A Play." The confused labels symbolize a shifting, changing, uncertain age, which liked novelty and was amused by a wide variety of dramatic themes and forms.

No matter how a Restoration dramatist defined tragedy, he had certain fixed notions about its nature, and, when he was at a loss for arguments, he could always cite the authority of Aristotle. Thus, in his essay "On the Grounds of Criticism in Tragedy" (1679) John Dryden felt obliged to paraphrase the Stagirite's definition of the genre as a topic sentence for his discourse. A tragedy, said Dryden, is "an imitation of one entire, great, and probable action; not told, but represented; which, by moving in us fear and pity, is conducive to the purging of those two passions in our minds." Expanding upon this definition, he pointed out that a tragedy must deal with a single action; it ought to have a natural order; "it ought to be great, and to consist of great persons, to distinguish it from comedy, where the action is trivial and the persons of inferior rank"; and "it ought to be probable as well as admirable and great." The purpose of tragedy, like that of all poetry, should be "to instruct delightfully."

This is very pretty, and pretty too is Dryden's subsequent discussion of the Manners, Characters, and Passions of the persons introduced into the fable — the story which was given life by the plot. In a number of prefaces and introductions, Dryden, a self-conscious artist who liked to parade his learning and justify his own plays, discussed the nature and purpose of tragedy in passages which reflect the best thinking of his age.

A representative pastiche of quotations should include the following: "To raise, and afterward to calm the passions, to purge the soul from pride by the example of human miseries which befall the greatest; in few words to expel arrogance and introduce compassion, are the great effects of tragedy." "The first rule . . . is to make the moral [the theme] of the work, that is, to lay down to yourself what that precept of morality shall be, which you would insinuate into the people. . . . 'Tis the moral that directs the whole action of the play to one center; and [the] action or fable is the example built upon the moral, which confirms the truth of it to our experience." Again, "All reasonable men have long since concluded that the hero of the poem [a tragedy] ought not to be a character of perfect virtue, for then he could not, without injustice, be made unhappy; nor yet altogether wicked, because he could not then be pitied. The characters which should move our pity ought to have virtuous inclinations and degrees of moral goodness in them." Finally, "In tragedy, where the actions and persons are great, and the crimes horrid, the laws of justice are more strictly observed [than in comedy]; and examples of punishment to be made, to deter mankind from the pursuit of vice." For Dryden, tragedy demanded belief in a morally ordered world and faith in a Divine Power which distributed even-handed justice.

Unfortunately Dryden never bothered to systematize his dramatic principles or to come down to the level of his readers. Expecting them to know, as he did, Aristotle, Horace, Longinus, Rapin, Le Bossu, Dacier, and Boileau, he saw no need to tell them that, according to the traditional concept of the genre, great, or high, tragedy dealt with an otherwise admirable protagonist who willfully broke a moral law and eventually expiated his sin, and that, in every case, the crime, the folly, or the infatuation of a tragic figure justified his fall. Nevertheless, he did his best to tell his fellow poets what great tragedy was and how to write it. When they refused to listen, he sneered at them for their "abominable fustian."

The epithet was well deserved. Most of Dryden's colleagues were butcherly hacks who thought of a tragedy simply as a serious play in the Elizabethan horror tradition, dominated by plot, with characters as so many pawns to be pushed about on a bloody chessboard. They equated tragedy with violent death. The more characters blinded, maimed, racked, raped, and murdered, the better the play, and, when the writer was at a loss for an ending, the kind "bowl" (goblet) of poison cleared the stage. Consequently, in a modern reader many Restoration tragedies provoke only pity for the actors who had to represent them and fear that they must have split their throats at the height of a resounding rant. Regrettably, not even the best writers — not even Dryden — were free from rants and fustian. We must not forget, however, that plays are designed to be produced in a theater, not to be read. Bombast can tickle the ears of the multitude, while the stage picture dazzles their eyes, and only the keenest critic can distinguish between noise and sense.

Because the Restoration audience liked to witness mayhem and murder, it is hard to find a tragedy without one or more killings on-stage. All the poets racked their brains for deadly devices more interesting than the commonplace sword and dagger. Pistols and muskets were unreliable engines and rarely used. Poison in a goblet of wine was convenient but conventional; some ingenious writers served their poison in skulls instead of glasses, or provided poisoned swords, daggers, baths, sweetmeats, or even poisoned gloves, one sniff of which was enough to send a victim into convulsions. Garroting with a silken cord was dramatically effective when it was done in full view of the audience. Beheading, hanging, and impaling were usually done off-stage, with appropriately horrid sound effects; when the scene opened the audience saw ghastly dummies in grotesque postures.

One objection to dramatic death by beheading, strangling, or hanging was that the victim lacked breath for a farewell speech. Stabbed through the lungs, he could die in verse, capping the final rhyme with his last breath. Lovers could take a long farewell; villains had time to confess and repent; and great men could philosophize on fate, chance, kings, and desperate men. If necessary, credibility was sacrificed to convention: for example, in Gould's *The Rival Sisters* (1695), wicked Catalina, *struck by lightning*, had time to confess her sins before she died. The dying speech became a screaming rant when the victim was poisoned. Apparently the poets were acquainted only with such irritant poisons as arsenic ("ratsbane"), which causes intense inflammation of the stomach and bowels. Thus the King of Sicily in Mountfort's *The Injured Lovers* (1688), dying from the effects of poison, cried,

> Give me some water there, some water, dogs;
> Pour down my throat a hundred thousand tuns
> To cool my boiling blood; let winter lay me
> In his frozen lap and weep snow on me;
> My heat would melt his board upon the Alps,
> And make a second flood for Italy.

Scenes exhibiting dead bodies were commonplace in every kind of tragedy. At the conclusion of Settle's *The Empress of Morocco* (1673), "the scene opens, and Crimalhaz [the villain] appears cast down on the gaunches, being hung on a wall set with spikes of iron." Payne's *The Siege of Constantinople* (1674) ends with a scene showing "a great number of dead and dying men in several manner of deaths. The Chancellor, Lorenzo, and Michael empaled." Elkanah Settle concluded *The Conquest of China* (1675) with this sweeping stage direction: "The scene opens, and is discovered a number of murdered women, some with daggers in their breasts, some thrust through with swords, some strangled, and others poisoned, with several other forms of death"—genus unspecified. In Dryden and Lee's *Oedipus* (1678) the "Scene draws and discovers Jocasta held by her women and stabbed in many places of her bosom, her hair dishevel'd; her children slain upon the bed." Ravenscroft added an exhibition to the horrors of *Titus Andronicus* (1679), "A curtain drawn discovers the heads and hands of Demetrius and Chiron hanging up against a wall. Their bodies in chairs in bloody linen." Crowne embellished the exhibition scene of *Darius, King of Persia* (1688) with a smartly dressed ghost, "The scene is drawn, and the carcasses of Bessus and Nabarzanes are seen, hung in chains, and stuck with darts, a guard attending. At another part of the stage is seen the ghost of Darius brightly habited." And at the end of D'Urfey's *The Famous History of Massaniello* (Part 2, 1699), "The scene opens and discovers the trunk of Massaniello, headless and handless, dragged by horses, his head and hands fastened to a pole, with an inscription, and behind them the bodies of Blowzabella, Pedro, and Pietro hanging upon gibbets."

Because bestial lust was a popular theme in tragedy, there are many cases of attempted rape, and some successful examples. Conventionally, like Roman Lucrece, the maid or matron who lost her virtue perforce could not long survive the event. (The obvious solution, a shotgun marriage for the maid and her ravisher, seems never to have occurred to the poets.) Stage directions descriptive of the hapless victim show that the conventional signs of rape were her disordered hair and gown. Thus in Ravenscroft's alteration of *Titus Andronicus,* "Enter . . . Lavinia, her hands cut off, and her tongue cut out, loose hair, and garments disordered, as ravished." In Brady's *The Rape* (1690), "The scene draws and discovers Eurione in an arbor, gagged and bound to a tree, her hair dishevelled as newly ravished, a dagger lying by her." At the end of the play she stabs herself. In Pix's *Ibrahim* (1696), Morena, who has been raped by the Sultan, is returned to her father, "her hair down, and much disordered in her dress." Morena makes her quietus with a bowl of poison.

Clearly sensationalism is the hallmark of Restoration tragedy in general. Other characteristics are: a plot with a "moral" —

a theme of love, lust, ambition, revenge, or villainy — which placed royal or noble characters with virtuous inclinations in dangerous situations and either saved or destroyed them; an attempt, rarely successful, to purge the passions with pity and terror; and a steady insistence upon the proper distribution of rewards for the virtuous and punishments for the wicked. Everything was designed to please an audience avid for sensation, excitement, and erotic titillation. As Nathaniel Lee, a successful tragic poet, remarked, "It is the business of poor poets to be the diversion of mankind; pleasure is their being." Lee's success was at least partly due to the fact that he heaped the stage with horrors.

Following the terminology of the age, we will have to call every kind of serious play a tragedy, whether it ends happily or unhappily. But we can distinguish four marked varieties: (1) villain, or intrigue, tragedy, which deals with lust, ambition, or revenge and places the emphasis upon a villain; (2) heroic tragedy, which is dominated by a character of heroic proportions; and has love-versus-honor as its theme; (3) high tragedy, which shows the fall of a great man who is destroyed by his own passions; and (4) pathetic, or sentimental, tragedy, which shifts the emphasis from villainy to the sufferings of innocent victims.

*** 7 ***

Villain Tragedy

WHEN THE KING'S and the Duke's companies were organized in the autumn of 1660, the two Masters, Killigrew and Davenant, got together and divided up the rich stock of older English plays, like two schoolboys choosing up sides. Thereafter, until they could begin harvesting crops of new plays, they presented only revivals of plays by the Elizabethan, Jacobean, and Caroline dramatists — "the giant race before the Flood" — plays which had been popular in the years immediately before the closing of the theaters in 1642. The best tragedies of Shakespeare were played, of course (most of them at the Duke's Theater), and the meaty comedies of Ben Jonson (at the Theater Royal), but the daily dramatic fare was made up largely of comedies and tragedies by Chapman, Webster, Massinger, Middleton, Beaumont and Fletcher, Ford, Brome, and Shirley. Davenant, who had been writing plays since 1627, had the pleasure of reviving most of his own dramas, and old Tom Killigrew, a very bad playwright, persuaded his actors to present at least three of his youthful effusions.

After the first few years, whenever a company was at a loss for a new play, it revived some long-forgotten romantic comedy or a blood-and-thunder intrigue tragedy, and whenever a hack playwright needed a plot he dusted off and altered some musty old play, brazenly presenting the resultant stepchild as his legitimate offspring. The spicy flavor of the old drama carried on to the new, as if there had never been a theatrical interregnum.

Because the members of the Restoration audience, like their predecessors in London's "private" theaters, were Court-oriented aristocrats, their tastes ran to tragedies set in Spain, France, Italy, Turkey, Persia, India, or any exotic land which could provide a royal court and a compost suitable for the growth of eroticism and intrigue. They were not interested in moralized calamities; they liked suspense stories, garnished with sex and sensuality. In short, they liked thrillers, but being royalists they preferred plays about the intrigues and dangers that perpetually beset a throne, the rise and fall of ambitious court favorites, and the delightful results of fornication and adultery in high places. The stories they enjoyed had no clearly local or contemporary application — although once or twice Mr. Pepys was a little worried about the King's reaction to a topical play. The Restoration poets took their plots and characters from old plays, from romantic fiction, or from equally romantic history. Their settings were unimportant; a given plot could be placed in any of a dozen foreign countries with the same results. The insular audience was very ready to believe that all kinds of monstrosities could thrive and grow in the decadent world beyond the tight confines of England.

Perhaps the commonest theme of Restoration villain tragedy is the rise of a scoundrel to power by means of lies, treachery, seduction, and murder. Eventually, of course, the villain gets his comeuppance, but not until he has worked his bloody will beyond the limits of credibility. The playwrights started with two basic assumptions: that some men and women are evil by nature, or can be easily turned to evil, and that all "good" people are credulous and not a little stupid. Perhaps they were right.

Consider, for example, Aphra Behn's successful *Abdelazer, or The Moor's Revenge* (1677), an alteration of a forgotten Elizabethan tragedy of blood, *Lust's Dominion, or The Lascivious Queen* (ca. 1600). Mrs. Behn largely rewrote the old play, smoothed out its crudities, dropped its comic characters, and added considerably to the sensuality and savagery of the original. She added also, rather incongruously, a pair of charming songs, and, to make the play seem modern, an occasional remark about "love and honor."

The arch-villain, Abdelazer, and his mistress, Isabella, Queen of Spain, dominate the action. Abdelazer was formerly the Prince of Fez. After his country's defeat by Spain and his father's death in battle, Abdelazer, then a youth, was brought up in the Spanish Court, promoted to the rank of general, and given a virtuous Spanish lady in marriage. Yet for years he has harbored fiendish thoughts of vengeance in his sooty breast. Moreover, he worships "Idol ambition," and would like to be King of Spain. But he really needs no motivation; like Barrabas in Marlowe's *The Jew of Malta* he is a natural villain, one who finds his greatest joy in mayhem and murder. At one point, after callously giving orders for a double murder, he soliloquizes,

> So, I thank thee, Nature, that in making me,
> Thou didst design me villain,
> Hitting each faculty for active mischief.
> Thou skillful Artist, thank thee for my face,
> It will discover nought that's hid within.
> Thus armed for ills,
> Darkness and horror, I invoke your aid.
> And thou, dread Night, shade all your busy stars
> In blackest clouds,
> And let my dagger's brightness only serve
> To guide me to the mark — and guide it so
> It may undo a kingdom at one blow.

As the play opens, Queen Isabella, to please her lover, has just poisoned her husband, old King Philip. Two sons survive, Ferdinand, the older, a soft-hearted, foolish young man who succeeds as King, and Prince Philip, the younger, a hot-headed, angry youngster, who is convinced that his mother has committed adultery with Abdelazer. But, because the new King is besottedly in love with Abdelazer's wife, he refuses to believe Philip's accusations. Free to continue his villainies, Abdelazer plots, unsuccessfully, to have Prince Philip and the powerful Cardinal Mendoza murdered, and tries to persuade his wife to murder the young King. But Florella is a true royalist:

> Murder my King! the man that loves me too —
> What fiend, what fury such an act would do?
> My trembling hand would not the weapon bear,
> And I should sooner strike it here — than there.
>
> *Pointing to her breast.*

But Abdelazer has no compunctions. He permits the jealous Queen to murder Florella, while with his own sword he slays the young King. Abdelazer is in control of the state, but arrayed against him are the armies of Cardinal Mendoza and Prince Philip. In hand-to-hand battle Abdelazer performs prodigies of valor. The Queen detaches Mendoza from Philip by promising him her love. (Strange, the power of love to ruin good men, even churchmen!) Abdelazer persuades the Queen to declare Philip illegitimate. The unnatural mother does so, and maliciously names Mendoza as his father. At last, after war, lies, treachery, and tricks, Abdelazer has all his enemies in his power. Since the Queen is no longer useful, he has her murdered, slays the assassin, declares Princess Leonora Queen of Spain, makes violent love to her, and is only by chance prevented from ravishing her.

To make sure of his enemies, Abdelazer sends his Moorish slaves to murder them in prison. But suddenly, "weary now of being a tyrant's slave," the captain of the Moorish guards turns honest and frees Philip, Mendoza, and Alonzo, a colorless young nobleman betrothed to Leonora. Quickly the tables are turned. Caught in a press of his enemies, Abdelazer, the "monstrous instrument of Hell," defies them, brags of his villainies, kills the renegade captain, and dies with half a dozen swords in his bowels. Since Philip is now hailed as King, and his sister Leonora gets to marry young Alonzo, the play may be said to have a happy ending. The butcher's bill comes to seven dead out of a cast of fifteen.

Although this is a better than average villain play, it falls far short of Dryden's standards for tragedy — even for that lesser sort "which end with a prosperous event." The action is single, but the persons are great only in the technical sense that they are kings and princes; only the villain has any superior qualities. It is difficult to discern a "moral," unless it be the admonition "Never trust a Moor." The highly improbable plot depends largely upon the gullibility of Abdelazer's victims, who are so many woodcocks to his springes. The crimes are sufficiently horrid, but they are committed by the villains, not by the protagonists. There is no great man whose fall can purge pride and move pity; instead we have the rise and fall of a monster, far too wicked to be pitied.

Mrs. Behn's characters are crudely simple. Dryden argued that "A character . . . cannot be supposed to consist of one particular virtue, or vice, or passion only; but 'tis a composition of qualities which are not contrary to one another in the same person." Mrs. Behn's method is largely characterization by epithet: "villain" Abdelazer, "love-sick" King Ferdinand, "hot-brained" Prince Philip, "jealous" Cardinal Mendoza, and the "lustful" Queen. When she tries to probe deeper into the minds of her creations, she comes up with nonsense. Thus Queen Isabella declares her libertinism in turgid couplets,

> Nature, be gone, I chase thee from my soul,
> Who Love's almighty empire does control;
> And she that will to thy dull laws submit,
> In spite of thee, betrays the hypocrite.
> No rigid virtue shall my soul possess,
> Let Gown-men preach against the wickedness;
> Pleasures were made by gods, and meant for us,
> And not t' enjoy 'em were ridiculous.

Mrs. Behn never allows her villains a moment of humanity, or her protagonists a moment of common sense.

Popular in its own time, *Abdelazer* was frequently revived until the end of the century. It had the theatrical merits of rapid, violent action, alarums and excursions, ranting, passionate speeches, blatant sexuality, and suspense. But the chances are that its initial success was due in large measure to the acting of Thomas Betterton as Abdelazer (in blackface and Moorish robe), to William Smith as Prince Philip, to beautiful, passionate Mary Lee as the evil Queen, and to pretty Mary Betterton as Florella. Elizabeth Barry, the rising star of the tragic stage, had the small part of Leonora. Many years later Betterton praised her for her ability to make even worse plays palatable — "she has often so exerted herself in an indifferent part that her acting has given success in such plays as to read would turn a man's stomach." Perhaps all the Restoration tragic actors had some measure of this skill — and often needed it.

Of the many other Restoration villain tragedies, few deserve even brief mention. On the whole they are (like many modern movies) crude, undigested melodramas, depending upon violent action and bloody show for their shock effect. For example, Thomas Porter's *The Villain* (1662) is dominated by an Iago-like scoundrel, "honest, honest Maligni." At the end of the play, the scene opens and we see "Malig. discovered pierced with a stake." Served him jolly well right; he was responsible for six deaths. Sir Robert Howard's *The Vestal Virgin, or The Roman Ladies* (1664), built on a confused love intrigue complicated by a pair of lustful villains, is equipped with two endings. In the tragic ending one character is blinded, five are killed, two commit suicide, and one is led off to execution. By ending it "the comical way," Howard preserved the lives and sight of all the protagonists, and killed only the villains. Henry Neville Payne's *The Fatal Jealousy* (1672), a Spanish intrigue monstrosity in blank verse, boasts of another Iago-like villain, Jasper, and a total of eleven dead out of a cast of thirteen. Lee's *Nero* (1674) show a selection from the more spectacular crimes of that homicidal maniac. Ten dead. Otway's *Alcibiades* (1675), by some critics considered a heroic play, deals far more with villain intrigue than with heroic love. Lustful Queen Deidamia and the villains Tissaphernes and Theramnes dominate the play until they all succumb to steel. There are so many deaths (six out of a cast of ten) that Mary Lee (Queen Deidamia), who spoke the prologue, confessed,

> Now who says poets don't in blood delight . . .
> Ours made such havoc that the silly rogue
> Was forced to make me rise for the epilogue.

The Popish Plot years (1678–1682) opened up a new source for villains. For example, in *Caesar Borgia* (1679) Lee depicted a decadent Italian world in which Roman Catholicism sanctioned lust, incest, and murder. Machiavel, the leading villain, escapes unscathed, but five people are strangled on-stage; one woman dies after sniffing at poisoned gloves; Borgia and Cardinal Ascano Sforza die of poison on-stage, while Pope Alexander is poisoned off-stage; and Borgia's little son is brought on "with his eyes out, and face cut," to die. In *The Female Prelate* (1680) Elkanah Settle retold the lurid myth of Pope Joan (Joanna Angelica), a lustful woman who hid her tiger's heart under priestly robes, rejoiced in the fine art of murder, and rose to the throne of St. Peter.

The brief reign of Catholic James II (1685–1688) put a temporary stop to intrigue tragedies with priestly villains. However, in *The Massacre of Paris* (written before 1682 but forbidden until 1689), Nathaniel Lee showed

> the most bloody rage
> That ever did religious fiends engage.

Huguenots are poisoned, stabbed, and shot, and the play ends with the execution of six Huguenot commanders on-stage by a firing squad, while "the scene draws" and shows the body of the Huguenot Admiral Chattillon in flames.

In the last years of the century, the poets turned to writing romantic villain tragedies again, but now with a new twist. Perhaps because of a strong drift toward feminism in drama, the villainess became the central figure and dominated the play. By a nice coincidence, three female playwrights were among the first to exploit the new sensation. In Catherine Trotter's *Agnes de Castro* (1695), Elvira, aided by her brother Alvaro, works her wicked mischief for revenge against Prince Pedro, who jilted her. Five dead. In Mary Manley's *The Royal Mischief* (1696), Homais, Princess of Libardian, is motivated by lust for Levan Dadian, Prince of Colchis. She gets him, and sets off a chain of villainies. Six dead — one is shot out of a cannon. In Mary Pix's *Ibrahim, The Thirteenth Emperor of the Turks* (1696), Sheker Para, the Sultan's chief mistress, is the villainess. When her lustful advances are rejected by General Amurat, who loves Morena, Sheker Para persuades the Sultan to ravish Morena. Morena's family seeks revenge. Result: seven dead, including the Sultan, Sheker Para, Morena, and Amurat.

Man's delight in villain melodramas seems to be universal. Critics in all ages have so often sneered at them as claptrap that "melodrama" has become a pejorative label. But melodramas still thrive on the modern stage and bid fair to continue. The subjects have shifted with the interests of each generation, but the basic ingredients have remained the same: rapid action, violent deaths and horrors, suspense, and a liberal dash of sex.

*** 8 ***

Heroic Tragedy

HEROIC TRAGEDY resulted from the attempt of the Restoration poets, led by John Dryden, to produce their own kind of poetic drama. It has been argued that heroic tragedy was the theater's response to an unheroic age, that the presentation of heroic figures in realistic plays would have made too painful a contrast between what was and what might have been, and that therefore the poets had to present their ideal heroes in Cloud-Cuckoo-Land. This interesting theory ignores one of the basic qualities of human nature — what we might call, after Thurber, the Walter Mitty syndrome — everyman's yearning for heroism.

Every child needs a hero, and most men long for a charismatic character, someone on a white horse to admire, if not to emulate. Without heroes, real or fictional characters whose spacious souls and mighty deeds make them seem larger than life, our daily lives would lack the spice of greatness. In the theater, by what Coleridge called "that willing suspension of disbelief for the moment, which constitutes poetic faith," we are able to accept the most remarkable stage hero as real — king, general, philosopher, scientist, detective, cowboy, physician, or full-back. We can love with him, fight and conquer with him, and glory in his triumphs. So long as he remains true to our concept of heroic virtue, our hero's downfall is unthinkable. He may be tempted, wounded, captured, and brought to the brink of ruin, but we expect him, in the long run, to win over the forces of evil, or, if by mischance he is slain, to die gloriously. This is poetic justice: good is properly rewarded — preferably here rather than in the hereafter — and evil is properly punished. We want our hero to live happily ever after with the woman he loves, and we want the villain to pay for his crimes.

The fictional heroes of any group or generation embody the characteristics most valued by that group from childhood to manhood. Restoration heroes were warriors because the aristocratic coterie considered war to be the noblest exercise of a gentleman; they were lovers because the coterie believed love to be the noblest frailty of the mind (as it was certainly the coterie's favorite indoor sport); and they were rulers or potential rulers because the seventeenth century still considered kingship to be man's greatest dignity. In *The Tragedies of the Last Age* (1678) Thomas Rymer argued, "We are to presume the greatest virtues where we find the highest of rewards; and though it is not necessary that all heroes should be kings, yet undoubtedly all crowned heads by poetical right are heroes." This was an extreme statement, but in the Restoration world it was at least politic. Lord Chamberlains were quick to pounce on antimonarchical sentiments in a play.

The members of the Restoration audience may not have been heroic in temper — the argument is moot — but they were assuredly nourished on war. Many men lived through a civil war, three separate wars with the Netherlands, the war of Monmouth's rebellion in 1685, the reconquest of Ireland, and the long war with France from 1689 to 1697. The Restoration had its share of heroic warriors: King Charles II, who had fought valorously for his throne; James, Duke of York, a brave admiral; dashing Prince Rupert; George, Duke of Albemarle, a doughty old warrior; Edward, Earl of Sandwich; James, Earl of

Ossory, a pattern of chivalry; Sir Christopher Mings; King William III, and dozens of admirals and generals.

With few exceptions, the gentlemen in any given audience were bred and trained for war. They had learned to use sword and pistol against highwaymen who wanted their purses, and against other gentlemen who impugned their honor. Many courtiers and wits held commissions in line regiments, the King's Guards, or the navy, and most country gentlemen were inept but willing officers in their county militia regiments. In time of war, if he was not already an officer, a gentleman joined a warship as a volunteer, or "reformado," and displayed his courage in the flaming hell of a sea battle. Even in times of peace some adventurous gentry volunteered to serve abroad in the endless continental wars, returning, bronzed and sabre-scarred, to the applause of their friends and the adoration of their doxies. To those who lacked stomach for battle, or who had had their fill of gunpowder, mud, and fever, or who had grown old and loved to recall the pomp and circumstance of past glories, the theaters offered a vicarious experience in the derring-do of a plumed player, who scattered flocks of scenekeepers with his blunted sword.

John Dryden argued that "an heroic play ought to be an imitation in little of a heroic poem; and consequently, that love and valor ought to be the subject of it." Largely because of his example, heroic tragedy, which flourished on the English stage from about 1664 to 1684, presented heroes with "virtuous inclinations and degrees of moral goodness," who bragged, ranted, made tempestuous love, defied the gods, and periodically tore a passion to tatters. These robustious, periwig-pated fellows were modeled on such heroes of history and fiction as Achilles, Alexander the Great, Marc Antony, Tasso's Rinaldo, and Calprenède's Artéban. They throve in romantic, faraway lands, and usually in the distant past. Like Marlowe's Tamburlaine they threatened the world "with high resounding terms" and scourged kingdoms with their conquering swords.

The external plot of a typical heroic play involved the godlike hero in war, revolution, or palace intrigue, and set him against powerful antagonists and seemingly hopeless odds. Trumpets blared, drums rumbled, gunpowder flashed, swords rattled, and sheep's blood drowned the stage to the great diversion of the spectators. The poets garnished their plays with songs, dances, and spectacular effects; their demands for scenes and machines taxed the resources of the theaters. Usually the poets wrote in heroic couplets, with due attention to balance, antithesis, and the jingle of rhyme. The actors spoke their lines in a musical cadence, or "heroic tone." As Elkanah Settle wrote of one playhouse in his preface to *Fatal Love* (1680), "The Theater Royal was once all harmony, and there the heroic muses sung so sweetly, and with voices so perfectly musical, as few or no ears could escape enchantment."

But the Restoration audience wanted also an internal conflict, something more than sound and sensation, something with a modicum of intellectual appeal. For this demand the poets had a ready answer. According to the romantic concept of greatness, as it was strained through French and Elizabethan sieves and blended with seventeenth-century psychology, only a hero was capable of "heroical love," and none but the brave deserved the fair. ("Love is a species of melancholy," wrote Robert Burton, in *The Anatomy of Melancholy*. "The part affected in men is the liver; and therefore called heroical because commonly gallants, noblemen, and the most generous spirits are possessed with it.") For an inner conflict the poets had only to show the protagonist in all the torments of a love-and-honor crisis.

This theme touched the lives of the aristocratic gentry, who liked to think of themselves as "the most generous spirits." The ladies, of course, could dream of yielding to the passion of a heroic lover. Many in the audience had heard the theme debated on the stage before the civil war — in such a play as Davenant's *Love and Honor* (1634), which in turn grew out of Beaumont and Fletcher's romantic tragicomedies — or more recently in France in the classical, declamatory plays of Corneille.

Many had read and enjoyed the long love-and-honor discussions in prose fiction, especially in the massive novels of Montemayor, Durfé, Calprenède, and Scudéry. (Mrs. Pepys was so fond of telling her friends long stories out of Scudéry's *Artamène ou le Grand Cyrus* that her husband had to silence her.)

Heroical love was an irrational passion, a distemper of the body humors which affected heart and mind; it represented a victory of the senses over the power to reason. The hero became a slave to his erotic passion, and no matter how outrageous his behavior, he was not to be held morally responsible. Honor was a blend of all the virtues appropriate to a gentleman. (Mere citizens and yeomen, of course, had no honor.) Upon the love-versus-honor theme the poets built their arguments, debating love versus chivalry, loyalty, duty, friendship, reason, martial pride, the demands of empire, and so forth. For a heroic play to have a happy ending, the poet had to bring head (reason) and heart (passion) to a resolution. Woe to the hero whose passion ruled his head and made him the slave of an unworthy love! His end was pitiful.

For the development of the love-and-honor theme, the hero had to fall headlong in love (usually at first sight) with an untouched heroine whose beauty was as irresistible as the hero's sword. The hero was expected to besiege his adored one passionately, with persuasive rhetoric, arguments, "whines," and threats of suicide. Swamped by a rolling flood of musical tones, the lady was expected to repress her own passion, to remain chaste and rational, and to remind the hero of his pride, his responsibility, and his greatness in battle. In the debate between two such war-crossed lovers, the poet racked his imagination for new arguments, and sometimes carried them to the heights of rarefied dialectic. After seeing Dryden's *The Conquest of Granada* Mrs. John Evelyn wrote to a friend, "Since my last to you I have seen 'The Siege of Grenada,' a play so full of ideas that the most refined romance I ever read is not to compare with it; love is made so pure and valor so nice that one would imagine it designed for an Utopia rather than our stage. I do not quarrel with the poet, but admire one born in the decline of morality should be able to feign such exact virtue; and as poetic fiction has been instructive in former ages, I wish this the same event in ours."

Dryden's *The Conquest of Granada,* which opened magic casements on the forlorn hills of Spain, was notably successful, but there is no reason to believe that it improved Restoration morality. Part One of the flamboyant, episodic play was presented on December 10, 1670, and Part Two on January 9, 1671. According to John Evelyn, it had "very glorious scenes and perspectives." Its heroics, its songs, and its "Zambra dance" made it a model for lesser writers to imitate. Almanzor, the hero, played in long coat, breeches, periwig, and high-plumed hat by Charles Hart, the handsome leading man of the King's Company, was so popular that "Almanzor" became a byword for a bombastic, all-conquering hero. He was everyman's dream of a legendary paladin. Almahide, the chaste heroine, was played in a French gown à la mode by pretty little Nell Gwyn, who had returned to the stage temporarily to bring her keeper, King Charles II, to terms. She was out of her calling in a tragedy, but she was everyman's dream of the perfect mistress.

Imported from Africa by Prince Abdalla to aid Moorish Granada against Spain, Almanzor (a prototype of the western "hired gun") promptly distinguishes himself at a bullfight by cutting off the head of a charging bull. His sword is so quick that the head "made imperfect bellowings as it went" to the ground. Immediately thereafter, by the sheer power of personality, he quells two warring factions in Granada, the Zegrys and Abencerrages, and makes them behave. Reveling in war, which he calls a "noble sport," he leads the Moors against the Spaniards and defeats them in a pitched battle.

Almanzor is royal by nature; his chivalric honor soars regally above mere common concepts of law or justice. When he enters in the first act the Abencerrages are losing their battle with the Zegrys. Almanzor promptly joins the Abencerrages, saying,

I cannot stay to ask which cause is best;
But this is so to me, because oppressed.

When Prince Abdalla asks his help to gain the crown of Granada, and argues that he has a better title to it than his older brother, Boabdelin, Almanzor replies impatiently,

It is sufficient that you make the claim;
You wrong our friendship when your right you name.
When for myself I fight, I weigh the cause,
But friendship will admit of no such laws. . . .
True, I would wish my friend the juster side,
But in the unjust, my kindness is more tried.

He is a great soul who can be tied to a cause only by others' kindness or his own interest. He is, he claims,

as free as Nature first made man,
Ere the base laws of servitude began,
When wild in woods the noble savage ran.

For more than two acts, Almazor lives up to his reputation:

Vast is his courage, boundless is his mind,
Rough as a storm, and humorous as wind.
Honor's the only idol of his eyes;
The charms of beauty like a pest he flies;
And, raised by valor from a birth unknown,
Acknowledges no power above his own.

Unfortunately, in Act III the noble savage meets Almahide, and beauty charms his mighty heart. Suddenly smitten, he cries,

Arms and the dusty field I less admire,
And soften strangely in some new desire;
Honor burns in me not so fiercely bright,
But pale as fires when mastered by the light.
Even while I speak and look, I change yet more,

And now am nothing that I was before.
I'm numbed and fixed and scarce my eyeballs move;
I fear it is the lethargy of love!

This is heroical love; it strikes like a thunderbolt and leaves its victim in a lethargy, with his normal faculties and energies suspended.

Like his prototype, Montezuma, in Dryden and Howard's *The Indian Queen* (1664), heroic Almanzor is frustrated in love (because Almahide is betrothed to Boabdelin, King of Granada) but invincible in war. He is so mighty that there is no physical suspense; we know that he will win every battle. Instead, we are kept in suspense as we wonder what he will decide to do.

Almanzor has opponents galore, but, as Almahide tells him sweetly, "heroes must still be opposed by some,/Or they would want occasion to o'ercome." First are the Spaniards, led by King Ferdinand and the Duke of Arcos. When Almanzor defeats and captures Arcos, chivalrously offers to free him, and is denied by King Boabdelin, he leads a revolt, unseats Boabdelin, and puts Prince Abdalla on the throne of Granada. When Abdalla refuses to give him Almahide in marriage, he revolts again, unseats Abdalla, and restores King Boabdelin. Almahide ends this game of musical thrones by finally rejecting Almanzor. Oh, she loves him passionately, but she is the soul of honor and must keep her plighted troth to King Boabdelin. Almanzor's arguments, pleadings, and whinings avail nothing against her honor's icy armor. Part One ends with parting looks o' both sides, and Almanzor heading back to Africa.

Meanwhile the two great families, the Zegrys and the Abencerrages, have periodically taken time off from the defense of Granada to carry on their own feud. Caught between love and family loyalty are two lesser heroic figures, gentle Osmyn (Almahide's brother), an Abencerrago, and pretty Benzayda, a Zegry. Osmyn, a noble, virtuous youth, spends most of his time following his chivalric code, which bids him "succor the distressed," and Benzayda spends hers trying to save Osmyn from the couple's feuding fathers, each of whom, for different reasons, wants to cut her sweetheart's throat.

Except for Benzayda, the Zegrys are a hard lot. Zulema, their chief, is a cynical scoundrel who scorns Virtue's "lean holy face," persuades Abdalla to seek the crown, and lusts bestially after Almahide — *he* does not love in Almanzor's "romantic way." Hamet, Zulema's brother and confidant, is merely weak, but Lyndaraxa, Zulema's sister, is a beautiful monster. She keeps two besotted lovers dangling: Prince Abdalla and Abdelmelech, chief of the Abencerrages. She is ambitious and frankly proclaims her willingness to marry any man who can make her a queen. She lies, cajoles, cheats, betrays, and pretends perfect innocence — "For I am sure I'm never in the wrong." In his futile attempts to win her love, Prince Abdalla loses his honor, his temporary throne, and finally his life. Even Abdelmelech, who understands her wiles, is helpless against her beauty.

Part Two brings Almanzor back from the coast, where he has been waiting for a ship. The Spanish forces are winning, and the Moors of Granada, "the many-headed beast," demand that King Boabdelin recall their hero, Almanzor. Here Dryden's "moral" for the play, "that union preserves a commonwealth, and discord destroys it," is reinforced by a corollary argument, that the common herd, misled by its leaders, can be dangerous. With an obvious glance at the tug-of-war between King Charles and the House of Commons in 1670, Dryden wrote,

> While people tug for freedom, kings for power,
> Both sink beneath some foreign conqueror;
> The subjects find too late they were unjust,
> And want that power of kings they durst not trust.

Almanzor returns. Now Almahide is married to King Boabdelin, and of course her husband, another victim of heroical love, is insanely jealous at the slightest favor she shows the hero. Almanzor does some unheroic sulking, and Almahide has to goad him into action against the Spanish besiegers. One night the hero's raging libido brings him to Almahide's bedroom door. He is warned off by his mother's ghost (a visitor from the Mountains of the Moon), and is brought back to reason by Almahide's threat of suicide. Later, aided by young Osmyn, he fights to save his mistress when she is accused of adultery with Abdelmelech; he kills her accusers, the villains Hamet and Zulema. Then the Zegrys, led by Lyndaraxa, betray the city to the Spaniards. In the course of a final battle, King Boabdelin dies with a Zegry sword in his heart, and heavenly voices warn Almanzor that the Duke of Arcos, with whom he is fighting, is his father. (Arcos recognizes his son by a birthmark and a ruby and diamond bracelet on his arm.) Abdelmelech, captured by Spanish soldiers commanded by Lyndaraxa, stabs the villainess and kills himself. Total slain on-stage, seven; off-stage, one king and a bull.

Now that Granada has been conquered by good Christians, and the villains — Zulema, Hamet, and Lyndaraxa — have been slain, the heroes must be rewarded. By their transcendent virtues Osmyn and Benzayda move their respective parents to sentimental tears, reconciliation, and permission to marry. Almanzor, now recognized as a grandee of Spain and nephew of King Ferdinand (we always knew he had royal blood in his veins), is to marry Almahide after her decent year of mourning. Heroic love has been justified, for

> Love's an heroic passion, which can find
> No room in any base, degenerate mind;
> It kindles all the soul with honor's fire,
> To make the lover worthy his desire.

The action of *The Conquest of Granada* is multiple rather than single, but it is certainly great. Granted the basic premises of heroic drama, the plot is probable enough; Dryden defended his romantic vision by pointing out that "an heroic poet is not tied to a bare representation of what is true, or exceeding probable." A neoclassic critic could complain that the unities of time, place, and action are blandly ignored. Dryden's answer might be that "the genius of the English cannot bear too regular a play; we are given to variety, even to a debauchery of pleasure." And here indeed is God's plenty. A monarchist might object that Almanzor treats King Boabdelin rather cavalierly, but it must be noted that Boabdelin is, in effect, a usurper. He had earlier sworn (and broken) an oath to resign his crown to King Ferdinand and live as a private man. Since he is not a true king he cannot be a hero "by poetical right." A soldier might argue that Almanzor's victories are improbable, but he should remember that in the seventeenth century generals fought shoulder to shoulder with their men, and many a battle was won by the stark courage and heroic example of a commander. A modern spectator, accustomed to low-keyed speeches and the cult of heroic modesty, might find Almanzor an insufferable braggart, but he should consider that the Restoration, like the Renaissance, expected its supermen to talk, as well as act, like Tamburlaines and Hotspurs. It was said of Almanzor,

> What, in another, vanity would seem,
> Appears but noble confidence in him;
> No haughty boasting, but a manly pride;
> A soul too fiery, and too great to guide;
> He moves eccentric, like a wandering star,
> Whose motion's just, though 'tis not regular.

Considering the play as a whole, and without pausing to quibble over such psychological crudities as heroical love and jealousy, one can find it good fun. The plots are well spun, the action is rapid, the characters are sharply defined, and the language is often vigorous. Dryden managed to comment on a variety of themes important to his audience; among them: love, honor, fate, virtue, kingship, and the dangers of mob rule and domestic disorders. It is, indeed, "a play so full of ideas that the most refined romance" is not to be compared with it.

But of course the play is not a tragedy, even though it offers two examples of those "human miseries which befall the greatest" — the destruction of the secondary characters Abdalla and Abdelmelech, both of whom loved unwisely and suffered for their folly. Sensitive observers may have felt pity and terror as they watched the futile struggles of two souls mired in the quicksand of unworthy love; and perhaps, if modern observers were not repelled by poetic drama, by the artificiality of Dryden's verse, they too would feel at least pity.

But for invincible Almanzor it is difficult to feel either pity or terror. He is too large-framed, too heroic to lose a battle or, except temporarily, a mistress. There is a moment when he seems destined to become a truly tragic figure. In Part Two, IV, 2, his erotic passion boils up and momentarily clouds his reason. It is late at night, and Almahide stands at her chamber door, no doubt "loosely dressed." Kneeling, Almanzor begs her to yield to "warm desire."

> ALMAHIDE. Rise, rise, and do not empty hopes pursue;
> Yet think that I deny myself, not you.
> ALMANZOR. A happiness so high I cannot bear;
> My love's too fierce, and you too killing fair.
> I grow enraged to see such excellence! —
> If words, so much disordered, give offense,
> My love's too full of zeal to think of sense.
> Be you like me; dull reason hence remove,
> And tedious forms, and give a loose to love.
> Love eagerly; let us be gods tonight;
> And do not, with half yielding, dash delight.

Had Almahide yielded we could have had high tragedy: the downfall of admirable protagonists who willfully break a moral law and must expiate their sin. But Dryden was not yet ready for high tragedy. Almahide, as passionate as her lover, retains her reason and all is well. In the last act the poet found a way to reconcile love and honor and to send his lovers to the holy bed of matrimony. In his later years Dryden (who had once sneered at happy endings) boasted, "Neither is it so trivial an undertaking to make a tragedy end happily; for 'tis more difficult to save than 'tis to kill. The dagger and the cup of poison are always in readiness; but to bring the action to the last extremity, and then by probable means to recover all, will require the art and judgment of a writer and cost him many a pang in the performance." Dryden was never afraid of the hobgoblin consistency.

To keep up the flow of heroic couplets and epic similes through the ten acts of *The Conquest of Granada* must have cost Dryden many a pang, too. He justified his choice of verse as a medium for heroic drama with the argument that because a heroic play was "an imitation in little of a heroic poem" it should be written in heroic verse. Moreover, heroic verse was necessary, he insisted, for the heightening of heroic characters; it was artistically appropriate so long as it was *good* verse. The argument was logical enough, but the results were not always happy.

Even granting Dryden's argument, we can complain that heroic verse, with its tight couplet structure, its antitheses and slapping rhymes, is an unhandy medium for the stage, even if the players delivered it in a kind of operatic recitative. The heroic couplet is effective in narrative, or as a medium for tightly reasoned argument or satire, but its wings are too clipped for romance and soaring passion. For example, when Almanzor ponders over man's fate, he speaks in admirably precise, sententious couplets:

> O Heaven, how dark a riddle's thy decree,
> Which bounds our wills, yet seems to leave them free.
> Since thy foreknowledge cannot be in vain,
> Our choice must be what thou didst first ordain.
> Thus, like a captive in an isle confined,
> Man walks at large, a prisoner of the mind;
> Wills all his crimes, while Heaven the indictment draws,
> And, pleading guilty, justifies the laws.
> Let fate be fate; the lover and the brave

> Are ranked, at least, above the vulgar slave.
> Love makes me willing to my death to run;
> And courage scorns the death it cannot shun.

But when Almanzor speaks in the swelling oratorical accents of passionate love, the couplets and triplets get in his way, and his stilted speeches are hollow. Banished by Almahide at the end of Part One, he says farewell to her:

> Like one thrust out in a cold winter's night,
> Yet shivering underneath your gate I stay;
> One look — I cannot go before 'tis day.
>
> *She beckons him to be gone.*
>
> Not one? — Farewell. Whate'er my sufferings be
> Within, I'll speak farewell as loud as she;
> I will not be outdone in constancy.
>
> *She turns her back.*
>
> Then like a dying conqueror I go;
> At least I have looked last upon my foe.
> I go — but if too heavily I move,
> I walk encumbered with a weight of love.
> Fain I would leave the thought of you behind,
> But still, the more I cast you from my mind,
> You dash, like water, back, when thrown against the wind.

By way of contrast, in Dryden's *All for Love,* which was written in flexible, emphatic blank verse, Antony banishes Cleopatra with "Hence from my sight forever!" Cleopatra replies,

> How? Forever?
> I cannot go one moment from your sight,
> And must I go forever?
> My joys, my only joys, are centered here.
> What place have I to go to? My own kingdom?
> That I have lost for you. Or to the Romans?
> They hate me for your sake. Or must I wander
> The wide world o'er, a helpless, banished woman,
> Banished for love of you — banished from you?

Aye, there's the banishment! Oh, hear me, hear me
With strictest justice, for I beg no favor,
And if I have offended you, then kill me,
But do not banish me.

ANTONY. I must not hear you.
I have a fool within me takes your part,
But honor stops my ears.

CLEOPATRA. For pity hear me!
Would you cast off a slave who followed you?
Who crouched beneath your spurn? — He has no pity!
See if he gives one tear to my departure,
One look, one kind farewell. O iron heart!
Let all the gods look down and judge betwixt us,
If he did ever love.

If Dryden had written *The Conquest of Granada* in blank verse, it might not have been a better play, but at least the dramatic idiom would have been happier — and more to the taste of a modern reader.

The demand for new heroic plays reached its meridian in the years 1675–1682 and thereafter set apace. The poets had searched through history and fable for heroes, and had deluged the stage with passionate lovers, chaste heroines, gullible kings, scheming villains, love-and-honor debates, and blood. Most of the productions of those years may be allowed to remain in well-deserved obscurity, but some are worthy of mention: Dryden's powerful *Aurenge-Zebe* (1675), Settle's bombastic *Ibrahim* (1676), Lee's *Mithridates* (1678), Crowne's lumbering two-part play, *The Destruction of Jerusalem* (1677), Bankes's *The Destruction of Troy* (1677) and *The Unhappy Favorite* (1681), and Southerne's *The Loyal Brothers* (1682). These are all readable, and some are delightful.

From its beginnings heroic drama had stirred up in the audience a small but active opposition party which detested and ridiculed heroics. For example, in September, 1664 (according to Mr. Pepys), Sir Charles Sedley witnessed a performance of Orrery's wooden heroic tragedy, *The General.* At one point the heroine, Altemira, commanded her suitor, Clorimun, to rescue his rival, Lucidor, whom she truly loved. After some demur, Clorimun cried to the audience,

> Well, I'll save my rival and make her confess
> That I deserve, while he do but possess.

"Why, what, pox," cried Sir Charles, the voice of Restoration cynicism, "what would he have him have more, or what is there more to be had of a woman than the possessing her?"

At another performance of the same play, when Lucidor, slightly wounded in fighting for his mistress, declared,

> This scratch, which you call wound, you much miscall,
> 'Tis my great trouble that it is so small,

we are told that George, Duke of Buckingham, rose in the pit and bellowed out,

> Then greater 'twere if it were none at all.

For years Buckingham was the leader of the opposition to heroic drama. In December, 1671, he and a trio of like-minded wits brought on the stage *The Rehearsal,* a burlesque of heroic tragedy, with Dryden satirized as Poet Bayes. Tradition has it that Buckingham coached the comedian John Lacy in the role of Bayes, dressed him in a suit of Dryden's clothes, and took the poet to the first performance to watch him squirm. Parts or passages from seventeen heroic plays were burlesqued, and Drawcansir, "a fierce hero that frights his mistress, snubs up kings, baffles armies, and does what he will without regard to numbers, good manners, or justice," became as much a byword as his model, Almanzor. *The Rehearsal* was frequently performed, and from time to time it was revised to keep it up to date.

In 1673, following the lead set by *The Rehearsal,* two university wits attacked Dryden and *The Conquest of Granada* in a pair of small prose pamphlets: *The Censure of the Rota on Mr. Dryden's Conquest of Granada* and *The Friendly Vindication of Mr. Dryden from the Censure of the Rota,* which was anything but friendly; it contained some sharp remarks on *Marriage à la Mode* and *The Assignation* as well as *The Conquest.* Later in the same year Joseph Arrowsmith, in a comedy, *The Reformation,* pictured Dryden in the character of the "Tutor to Pacheco," a fop. The Tutor is a foolish playwright, who tells his friends how he writes a tragedy. "I take a subject," he says, "as suppose the siege of Candy or the conquest of Flanders. . . . Then, sir, I take you some three or four or half a dozen kings. . . . As, sir, you must always have two ladies in love with one man, or two men in love with one woman; if you make them the father and the son, or two brothers or two friends, 'twill do the better. There, you know, is opportunity for love and honor and fighting and all that. . . . Then, sir, you must have a hero that shall fight with all the world; yes, i' gad, and beat them too, and half the gods into the bargain if occasion serves. . . . Last of all be sure to raise a dancing, singing ghost or two, court the players for half a dozen new scenes and fine clothes . . . put your story into rhyme, and kill enough at the end of the play, and, *probatum est,* your business is done for a tragedy."

Sneers, slighting remarks, burlesques, and satires had no perceptible effect on the popularity of heroic plays. With ordinary human inconsistency, the Restoration audience could enjoy a heroic play on a given afternoon, and could enjoy just as much a burlesque of heroics the very next afternoon. But the vogue for any specialized dramatic genre must wear itself out at last. It seems that the production of new heroic plays fell off after 1682 because the poets could find no more changes to ring on the love-and-honor theme. Finally, in his preface to *Don Sebastian* (printed in 1690), Dryden himself admitted that "love and honor (the mistaken topics of tragedy) were quite worn out." For many years the best heroic plays reappeared regularly on the stage, but the popular playwrights turned to new themes and forms.

*** 9 ***

High Tragedy

"TRAGEDY," said Milton, "as it was anciently composed, hath ever been held the gravest, moralest, and most profitable of all other poems." A good high tragedy — a play which shows a worthy protagonist destroyed by his own passions and the circumstances in which he is placed — is rare in any age, perhaps because only a great poet can reach such austere heights. The writer of high tragedy is not necessarily a pessimist; he is, rather, a serious artist who recognizes that certain human problems are not to be solved by the application of reason, common sense, or even psychiatry, and that human nature is vulnerable to the forces of evil within man himself. As George Meredith put it,

> In tragic life, God wot,
> No villain need be! Passions spin the plot;
> We are betrayed by what is false within.

Indispensable for a high tragedy is a protagonist who, if not great or heroic, is at least in some sense admirable, so that the breakdown of his personality and the inevitability of his doom will strike us with terror, and his impotence and suffering will move us to pity. This character must be shown in a situation to which, like most men of good will, he is vulnerable, so that he can cry, with Hamlet,

> The time is out of joint. Oh, cursed spite,
> That ever I was born to set it right.

Sometimes the protagonist is placed in a tragic dilemma; he must choose between two courses of action, each of which will inevitably lead to his doom. The unfolding of the tragedy must not depend upon chance or contrived devices, but upon those impulsive, passionate, or mistaken decisions and actions which are appropriate to the protagonist's character. A truly wise man — if one ever lived — would be no subject for high tragedy. A fool would be fit for pathetic tragedy only.

High tragedy usually ends with the protagonist's death, not because death in itself is tragic, but because it puts an end to a life which has become unbearable. As King Lear lay dying, and Edgar was solicitous to aid him, the Earl of Kent protested,

> Vex not his ghost. Oh, let him pass! He hates him
> That would upon the rack of this tough world
> Stretch him out longer.

The Restoration attitude toward high tragedy is shown, at least in part, by its response to some of Shakespeare's greatest plays. *Hamlet* and *Othello,* cut, but otherwise unaltered, were frequently performed, and Hamlet was Thomas Betterton's greatest role. *Julius Caesar* appeared on the stage from time to time, essentially unchanged. However, *Macbeth* was reduced to an opera, with songs, scenes, machines, and a dance of witches. *King Lear* was turned into a villain tragedy with a happy ending: Lear and Cordelia survived, and Cordelia married Edgar. Dryden himself turned *Troilus and Cressida* into a villain tragedy by making the Greek Diomedes swear falsely that he has enjoyed faithful, loving Cressida, who, rejected by Troilus, promptly kills herself. *Romeo and Juliet* and *Timon of*

Athens were each pillaged to make a London holiday. *Richard II* and *Coriolanus* became pathetic tragedies.

These were not mere wanton changes. The Restoration playwrights had their reasons: to improve the *liaison des scènes* and tighten up the plots, to "correct" Shakespeare's archaic and too figurative language, to distribute poetic justice, to modernize out-of-date themes, and to fit the old plays to audiences which liked happy endings, villain plays, and pathetic tragedies. Sometimes they reduced Shakespeare's "native woodnotes wild" to the piping of a penny whistle.

How fully the aristocrats in the pit and boxes appreciated Shakespeare's tragedies is a question not readily answered—perhaps they found some of them too grave and moral; perhaps the cynical or skeptical mind is incapable of enjoying Shakespearean tragedy. At least there are abundant critical testimonies to Shakespeare's greatness as a tragic writer. When Thomas Rymer attacked him in *The Tragedies of the Last Age* (1678), John Dryden accused Rymer of blasphemy. To Dryden and his friends, Shakespeare, with all his faults, was "the man who of all modern and perhaps ancient poets had the largest and most comprehensive soul."

Nathaniel Lee, who wrote a number of villain, heroic, and pathetic tragedies, had a large and comprehensive soul, and at least once climbed to the plateau of true tragedy. In spite of its highly emotional style, *The Rival Queens* (March, 1677) is an excellent blank verse tragedy. Lee took his basic plot from Calprenède's popular romantic novel, *Cassandre*, added elements from classical historians, and presented in the scope of a single day events which were historically years apart.

The title is misleading; in its own day the play was usually called "Alexander the Great" after its protagonist. Although Alexander's two wives, Statira and Roxana, are rivals for his love, and fierce Roxana murders Statira, who dies "so fair, so innocent, so young," Lee makes it clear that the murder is the direct result of Alexander's inability to control his passions. He is a victim of "heroical love" for a wicked woman.

To persuade Statira to marry him, Alexander had sworn that he would "never bed Roxana more," but, sometime after he married Statira, when he was at Susa and flushed with wine, he "relapsed and, conquered by Roxana's charms," took her to his bed. The results are that Roxana is pregnant, and Statira, mortally offended, swears that she will never again be a wife to Alexander. Alexander apologizes and pleads, Statira relents, Roxana stabs her, Statira dies, and Alexander mourns,

> Oh, she is gone, the talking soul is mute!
> She's hushed — no voice, no music now is heard!
> The bower of beauty is more still than death;
> The roses fade, and the melodious bird
> That waked their sweets has left them now forever.

There is nothing left to live for. When he hears, almost immediately, that his "dear Hephestion" is also dead, he moans,

> Alas, the dear
> Unhappy youth! But he sleeps happy,
> I must wake forever. This object, this,
> This face of fatal beauty,
> Will stretch my lids with vast, eternal tears.

He has only a short time for eternal tears. Presently, poisoned by a shabby lot of conspirators, he dies in conventional madness, with a bolt of ice hissing through his bowels.

In brief, Lee shows us the last stages in the disintegration of a once admirable protagonist, a heroic lover who "curls like a vine and touches like a god," but cannot resist temptation. He breaks his pledged word, gives way to lust, and releases a tempest of hate and jealousy which destroys his true love. "Headlong Alexander" is a world conqueror who once was modest but is now a blatant boaster, who once was reasonable and restrained, but now orders a physician crucified, throws an old friend to the lions, and in a rage slays his faithful general,

Clytus, with a javelin. Alexander's passion spins the plot to its inevitable conclusion. Without precise statement, Lee's "moral" seems to have anticipated Lord Acton's dictum: "All power tends to corrupt; absolute power corrupts absolutely." Alexander's spectacular death merely ends the tragedy of personal destruction — no villain need be.

Like all of Lee's plays, *The Rival Queens* seems to burst with energy. The characters are never at rest; they are in agonies of pain or ecstasies of bliss, and every speech seems to be screwed to the highest pitch of passion. Alexander Radcliffe, in *News from Hell* (1681), sneered at Lee as one

> whose lofty fancy towers
> 'Bove fate, eternity, and powers,
> Rumbles in the sky, and makes a bustle,
> So gods meet gods i' th' dark and justle.

But the secret of Lee's theatrical success was his lofty fancy, his ability to frame images of such cosmic scope that his enraptured audience, swept from its benches, was hurled headlong into ethereal skies. Lee's characters walk with the gods; their heads touch heaven, and their voices rise above the music of the spheres. For example, on his first appearance, Cassander, leader of the conspirators, who dares attempt the life of a demi-god, declaims,

> The morning rises black, the low'ring sun,
> As if the dreadful business he foreknew,
> Drives heavily his sable chariot on;
> The face of day now blushes scarlet deep,
> As if it feared the stroke which I intend,
> Like that of Jupiter — lightning and thunder!
> The lords above are angry and talk big,
> Or rather walk the mighty cirque like mourners
> Clad in long clouds, the robes of thickest night,
> And seem to groan for Alexander's fall.

"Jealous, bloody" Roxana rails in resounding terms, crying,

> My brain is burst, debate and reason quenched,
> The storm is up, and my hot bleeding heart
> Splits with the rack, while passions, like the winds,
> Rise up to heaven and put out all the stars.

Again, she cries that her "soul is pent and has not elbow room,"

> Oh that it had a space might answer to
> Its infinite desire, where I might stand
> And hurl the spheres about like sportive balls!

But when it comes to playing with the spheres, Alexander is the master. Rejected at first by Statira, he declares that he will rid himself of love:

> Yes, I will shake this Cupid from my arms,
> Drown him in the deep bowl of Hercules,
> Make the world drunk and then, like Aeolus,
> When he gave passage to the struggling winds,
> I'll strike my spear into the reeling globe
> To let it blood, set Babylon in a blaze,
> And drive this god of flames with more consuming fire.

These are examples not of rant but of rhapsody, of poetic fury; the concepts are as large as their expression. Even the most jaded playgoer must have been carried away by the sheer violence and audacity of Lee's images. But there were always sober men who had no love for poetry. In 1684, when Lee went violently insane and had to be confined (for four years) in Bethlehem Hospital, dour Anthony Wood noted in his *Diary*, "Nathaniel Lee, the playmaker, endeavoring to reach high in expression in his plays, broke his head and fell distracted."

Lee's friend and occasional collaborator, John Dryden, may have had a less comprehensive soul, but he had a more disciplined mind. For nearly three centuries critical opinion has agreed that Dryden's *All for Love, or The World Well Lost* (December, 1677) is the best example of Restoration high tragedy. It is not an alteration of Shakespeare's lusty, episodic *Antony and Cleopatra*, although Dryden borrowed, or adapted, a few passages from the earlier play. For example, he pruned and trimmed Enobarbus' florid description of Cleopatra as she came down the Nile in her barge, changing its archaisms and deleting its pathetic fallacies to fit the Restoration taste for the language of direct statement. Thus Enobarbus' verdict on Cleopatra —

> Age cannot wither her, nor custom stale
> Her infinite variety. Other women cloy
> The appetites they feed, but she makes hungry
> Where most she satisfies—

became in Dryden's hands Antony's "refined" apostrophe to his mistress,

> There's no satiety of love in thee:
> Enjoyed, thou still art new; perpetual spring
> Is in thy arms; the ripened fruit but falls
> And blossoms rise to fill its empty place,
> And I grow rich by giving.

Dryden glossed over the conclusion of Enobarbus' description

> For vilest things
> Become themselves in her, that the holy priests
> Bless her when she is riggish.

Dryden's Cleopatra was never wanton.

Further verbal comparisons would be odious. Shakespeare dramatized the entire Antony and Cleopatra story as told by Plutarch, while Dryden concentrated on the final events in the tale, after Antony's defeat by Octavius Caesar at Actium. In conformity with the neoclassic unities and the vogue for heroi plays, Dryden limited the action to a single straightforward conflict between love and honor — or reason. To achieve unity of place he set the action in one catch-all building, the Temple of Isis, and by carefully avoiding any mention of time he managed to give the impression that the ideal time of the play was not more than the permissible twenty-four hours. The neoclassic critics objected to the delightful slanging match between Cleopatra and Octavia as indecorous because both were great characters of high rank. With sublime common sense Dryden replied that, though one was a Roman and the other a queen, "they were both women."

In *All for Love* we see the final downfall of Antony, who, as played by Charles Hart, a veteran hero, is now the mere "shadow of an emperor"; he has almost lost his ability to reason and decide. ("Your bravest soldiers and most generous spirits," said Robert Burton, "are enervated with [love].") Dryden, a master plotter, worked out his conflicts and climaxes with almost mathematical precision. Thus in Act I, honest Ventidius, the embodiment of honor and reason, persuades Antony to leave Cleopatra and join twelve loyal legions waiting for him in Syria. Alexandria is besieged by Caesar, but there are still ways open. In Act II, Cleopatra, whose love is "a noble madness," persuades Antony to remain with her, and Ventidius complains,

> O women! women! women! all the gods
> Have not such power of doing good to man
> As you of doing harm!

In Act III, Ventidius, aided by Antony's wife, Octavia, and their two children, and by Antony's young friend, Dolabella, persuades Antony to desert Cleopatra and make peace with Caesar. In a contrived but very effective scene, Antony stands alone, stage center. His two little daughters run to him and throw their arms about him. Then —

> VENTIDIUS. Was ever sight so moving? — Emperor!
> DOLABELLA. Friend!

OCTAVIA. Husband!
CHILDREN. Father!
ANTONY. I am vanquished. Take me,
Octavia — take me, children — share me all.
Embracing them.
I've been a thriftless debtor to your loves,
And run out much, in riot, from your stock,
But all shall be amended.

In Act IV, nobody wins. On the advice of her prime minister, the eunuch priest Alexas, Cleopatra tries to make Antony jealous of Dolabella and succeeds all too well. Octavia, angered at Antony's concern for "an abandoned, faithless prostitute," flings away in a huff, breaking off negotiations with Caesar; and, in a fury, Antony rebuffs both Cleopatra and Dolabella. Now he is left with only faithful Ventidius to share his wretchedness.

In Act V, the Egyptian fleet deserts to Caesar. Antony and Ventidius have just decided to sally out with the remnant of their forces and die bravely in battle, when Alexas, carrying out another scheme to reunite the lovers, brings the false news of Cleopatra's death. Completely unmanned, Antony cries,

My torch is out; and the world stands before me
Like a black desert at th' approach of night.
I'll lay me down and stray no farther on.

Ventidius, called on to slay his master, instead kills himself. Antony falls on his sword. Cleopatra and her women find him dying, and seat him in a chair. He sings his swan song in melodious blank verse, dies, and Cleopatra, with her basket of "aspics," quickly follows him in death. As a mob enters the temple, they see the lovers seated together in somber state. Serapion, a priest, pronounces their benediction:

Sleep, blest pair,
Secure from human chance, long ages out,
While all the storms of fate fly o'er your tomb;

> And fame to late posterity shall tell,
> No lovers lived so great or died so well.

All for Love is soundly plotted, the characters are fully developed, and the verse is dramatic, vigorous, and flexible. The conflict is between love and reason, heart and head. At the beginning of the play Antony has lost his reason; he has disgraced "the name of soldier with inglorious ease." It is Ventidius' function to make him see his plight rationally and to act according to the dictates of reason. But Ventidius can never be sure of his pupil, who acts, now rationally, now impulsively, as his passions spin the plot. Cleopatra, urged by her maids to call reason to her aid, replies that she has none, "and none would have." She has loved "with such transcendent passion" that she has soared "quite out of reason's view" and now is lost above it. She is incapable of thought and depends on scheming Alexas to prescribe her course of action. Antony, destroyed by his own passions and the situation in which he is placed, is a truly tragic figure. Cleopatra, the embodiment of love, whose being depends on Antony's, and who prefers death with him to life without him, is merely pathetic.

Lacking a Greek chorus to remind us of Antony's former greatness, Dryden does his best with the means at hand. To Ventidius, Antony, before his love for Cleopatra ruined him, was "the lord of half mankind," the "bravest soldier and the best of friends," and "the chief and best of human race." To Ventidius he is still a "vast soul," "all that's good and godlike." To Dolabella, Antony is still "lord of all the world." To Cleopatra he is lover, lord, and hero, a "greater Mars." Antony himself reminds us of his former greatness, when he was "the wish of nations," and "the meteor of the world." Once he brags of the time when he stormed the heights before Cassius' camp so eagerly that he won the trenches single-handed, while his soldiers "lagged on the plain below." These constant reminders enlist our sympathy and admiration for a former hero.

One might complain that by taking Antony in his last hours,

Dryden has lost some of the terror aroused by the progressive decay of a tragic protagonist. As the play opens, Antony is already so far sunk in the lethargy of love that his flashes of strength seem like the false shows of health in a dying consumptive. But neoclassic limitations gave little space for slow decline, and if terror is diminished, pity is increased by the exposure of Antony's weakness and suffering.

No doubt *All for Love* is a magnificent tragedy, and yet — perhaps it is a little too pat, too well contrived, too coldly classical in form and style. Possibly the conflict is too mechanically balanced, the "moral" too obvious. "The chief persons represented," said Dryden in his preface to the play (printed in 1678), "were famous patterns of unlawful love; and their end accordingly was unfortunate." Yet, as his second title, *The World Well Lost,* suggests, Dryden hedged on his thesis. He seems to ask us, in effect, to forgive his lovers' faults and to blame their fate on the circumstances of their world. The "famous patterns of unlawful love" are not presented as sinners or adulterers; indeed, the word "sin" appears in connection with them only once in the play, when Octavia accuses Cleopatra of owning "those black endearments that make sin pleasing." Adultery is never mentioned.

There is no apparent moral problem. Political necessity forced Antony to marry Octavia (Caesar's sister) after the death of his first wife, Fulvia. He never loved Octavia; he loved only Cleopatra, whom Dryden depicts, not as the "serpent of old Nile," but as a sweet, good, beautiful woman meant by Nature to be a wife, "a silly, harmless, household dove." (The role was created by blonde Betty Boutell, an ingénue!) Cleopatra is aware that she has lost her honor and "stained the glory" of her royal house "to bear the branded name of mistress," but Antony seems unaware that he has done anything wrong, that he has broken a moral law and must pay the penalty. Instead he blames his own sloth and the gods, crying in his despair, "Is there one god unsworn to my destruction?" In the final scene, as the blood drains from his body, he whispers to Cleopatra,

> Think we have had a clear and glorious day,
> And Heaven did kindly to delay the storm
> Just till our close of evening. Ten years' love,
> And not a moment lost, but all improved
> To the utmost joys — what ages have we lived!
> And now to die each other's; and, so dying,
> While hand in hand we walk in groves below,
> Whole troops of lovers' ghosts shall flock about us,
> And all the train be ours.

From Antony there is no word of remorse, regret, or repentance. At the end of the play, we are not quite sure where the poet stands. Are the lovers punished for their sins, or is the world indeed well lost for such a love? Is their destruction the fault of a conventional world which privately approves "patterns of unlawful love" and publicly condemns them? Unlawful love was so common at the Court of Charles II that once Lord Chancellor North, a sober lawyer, was advised "that he should keep a whore . . . because he was ill looked upon for want of doing so." Remembering that there must have been dozens of well-known mistresses in the Restoration audience, and dozens of known keepers — including that insatiable sinner, King Charles — one can only wonder if Dryden was trimming his tragic sails to the winds of coterie opinion. No dramatist can rise above the tastes and prejudices of his audience.

If Thomas Otway's passion, pathos, and comprehensive soul had been supported by Dryden's judgment and constructive skill, Otway might have been indeed, as his admirers claim, "next to Shakespeare." Yet, careless plotter though he was, leaving loose ends flying in all directions, Otway wrote what was held to be in its own time and for generations thereafter the most moving tragedy of the seventeenth century, *Venice Preserved* (February, 1682). A brooding, sensitive, unhappy man, Otway left Oxford without taking a degree, failed as an actor, and became a playwright. He knew the degradation of poverty, the misery of military life (in 1678), and the bitterness of unrequited love for a worthless woman. He knew all the depths of human passion, if not the heights.

The source of Otway's plot in *Venice Preserved* was *Le Conjuration des Espagnolles contre la République de Venise en l'année MDCXVIII*, by César Vichard, Abbé de Saint-Réal, a narrative which was translated into English in 1675, with a second edition in 1679. Otway had quarried Saint-Réal before, dramatizing his novel *Dom Carlos* as *Don Carlos, Prince of Spain* (1676). Very probably the Popish Plot of 1678 inspired Otway to look into Saint-Réal's story for material for a tragedy. In the troubled years following Titus Oates's "discovery" of the Popish Plot, any play about any kind of plot was sure to be a success, a "natural."

In Saint-Réal's narrative, the Marquis de Bedmar (or Bedamar), the Spanish ambassador to Venice, has sharked up a list of lawless resolutes with whose aid he hopes to destroy Venice and make the power of Spain supreme in the Adriatic. From Saint-Réal's account of Bedamar's conspiracy, Otway drew his group of multinational soldiers of fortune, who were paid by Bedamar and were nominally headed by Nicolas Renault, an aged Frenchman of blameless life who took part in the plot in the hope of making his name immortal. Two of the leading mercenaries were Captain Jean Pierre, a Norman, formerly a successful pirate (usually referred to as "the Captain"), and his friend Anthony Jaffier, a soft-hearted Provençal who betrayed the plot to the Venetian Senate. Also involved in the original story were Anthony Priuli, a Venetian senator, and a nameless Greek courtesan (Acquilina in Otway's version), in whose house most of the conspirators lodged.

To Otway the story of Jaffier must have seemed a challenging problem in dramatic psychology. All he knew about Saint-Réal's Jaffier was that his imagination, painting for him in lurid colors all the horrors attendant upon an uprising, drove him to inform against his friends, at the same time insisting upon the

Senate's sacred promise to spare the lives of the twenty-two conspirators whom he named. (Later the Senate broke its word.) Otway was always fascinated by sensitive characters who were the victims of their own emotions and their too vivid imaginations. Yet to a Restoration dramatist a conflict between compassion and friendship would have seemed unsatisfactory as a tragic theme — the seventeenth century was not noted for humanitarianism.

In some fashion Otway had to turn Jaffier's problem into a love-and-honor conflict. Moreover, there had to be a role for Elizabeth Barry, the rising star of the Duke's Company, with whom Otway was said to be infatuated, and for whom he had recently written the pathetic role of Monimia in *The Orphan.* With the great Thomas Betterton as Jaffier and Elizabeth Barry playing opposite him, the play would have an excellent chance for success. Therefore Otway invented a wife for Jaffier, Belvidera, the embodiment of tender conjugal love. He invented also the lecherous old senator Antonio, whose scenes with the courtesan, Acquilina, are realistic studies of abnormal sex.

To secure our admiration for Jaffier and to give him an honorable motive for joining the plot against Venice, Otway remodeled the character, keeping only the surname. His Jaffier is a noble young Venetian of small, but adequate, fortune. He had been a very promising youth, and had shown his heroism by rescuing Belvidera, daughter of the rich senator Priuli, from the Adriatic waves. (This was no small feat in a world of nonswimmers.) Later, overcome by heroical love, Jaffier made the mistake of marrying Belvidera clandestinely, without her father's consent. This was the beginning of his downfall. Priuli was a typical father; the Restoration audience would not need to be told that he had hoped to arrange a marriage for his daughter which would increase his family's wealth and power. Rightfully incensed, Priuli disowned and disinherited Belvidera.

At the beginning of *Venice Preserved,* Jaffier, whose pride and love for Belvidera have made him squander his small fortune to maintain his wife and his infant son in state for the three years of his marriage, comes to Priuli for help, and gets only curses. "Cruel" Priuli deserves the epithet, but impulsive Jaffier was first at fault. As he is leaving Priuli's door, Jaffier meets his friend Pierre and learns that Belvidera has been turned into the street and all his goods have been seized by his creditors. To enlist our sympathy, Otway describes this as an act of wanton brutality, and tells us (through Pierre) that "Priuli's cruel hands" signed the bailiff's warrant (as a magistrate, Priuli could do no less). Now Jaffier is at the nadir of his fortunes and a fit subject for Pierre's purposes. Pierre urges revenge for "Belvidera's tears," and agrees to meet Jaffier at midnight for further talk.

Pierre (now presented as a soldier formerly in the service of Venice) is more villain than hero. Although he has his own code of honor, he is a cynic, a materialist who sneers at honesty as a cheat invented by fools and cowards. He is a soldier of fortune, whose excuse for engaging in a plot against Venice is the fact that, in his absence, wealthy Senator Antonio bought the favors of Pierre's mistress Acquilina (the Greek courtesan of Saint-Réal), and that when Pierre threw the old goat out of Acquilina's house, the Senate reprimanded him "for violating something they call 'privilege.'" These are very poor excuses for plotting revolution and murder. Pierre is no patriot seeking the reformation of a political and economic system. True, he speaks the routine cant of the doctrinaire revolutionary and calls for "liberty," but he is a hired bravo and what he really wants is loot, blood, and destruction. As he envisions the burning of Venice, he cries,

> How lovely the Adriatic whore,
> Dressed in her flames, will shine! — devouring flames,
> Such as shall burn her to the watery bottom
> And hiss in her foundation.

Keeping his appointment, Jaffier comes to the Rialto at midnight. He has lodged Belvidera privately (apparently in Acquilina's "house of fair reception") until he sees what fortune holds in store for him. He comes upon the stage with "all hell" in his heart, and calls upon the powers of darkness to meet him, crying aloud, "Hell! Hell! why sleepest thou?" Promptly on cue, Pierre enters to greet his proselyte. A few speeches later Pierre gives his friend a handful of the gold for which, at the moment, Jaffier is willing to sell his soul. Aside Jaffier says,

> I but wished
> To see the devil, and he's here already. — Well,
> What must this buy: rebellion, murder, treason?
> Tell me which way I must be damned for this.

By a nice irony he has hit upon the truth, but he doesn't recognize it. He trusts Pierre completely, and is sure that his dear friend would never lead him into "a villainous, inglorious enterprise."

Pierre's motives for bringing Jaffier into the Spanish plot to overthrow Venice seem to be double: to add another desperate, courageous man to the small band of conspirators and to give his friend a chance to recoup his fortunes. Although he continues to prate of liberty, he offers Jaffier material rewards:

> Thou shalt be freed from base Priuli's tyranny,
> And thy sequestered fortunes healed again.

But Jaffier barely hears him, and he ignores the insinuation of "sequestered," a word which suggests that his fortune had been seized by arbitrary authority. Full of bitterness and self-pity, Jaffier is intent only upon revenge for all his "wrongs." Having sworn an oath "by all good powers above, and ill below," and "by love and friendship," never to tell what Pierre is about to reveal, he is led off to a meeting of the conspirators at Acquilina's house. Jaffier leaves the stage crying for revenge. "And liberty!" Pierre warns, but Jaffier's reply is only "Revenge! Revenge!"

Now the plot of the play falters into improbability. Brought before the assembled conspirators, Jaffier, using Pierre's inflammatory phrases, talks boldly of his eagerness to "restore justice and dethrone oppression," to "cut the throats of reverend rogues in robes," and to "bear a lighted torch at noon" to fire the arsenal. Finding his auditors still skeptical, he summons Belvidera, who enters as if just out of bed. Jaffier turns her over to old Renault as a hostage, and with her the dagger which reappears later as the symbol of his pledged faith. If he proves unworthy of his trust, the dagger is to be sheathed in Belvidera's bosom. (Whatever became of Belvidera's infant son?)

At last the conspirators accept Jaffier as a comrade. Blindly believing Pierre, Jaffier thinks himself part of a truly noble enterprise, and is convinced that his new friends are

> men of souls, fit to reform the ills
> Of all mankind. There's not a heart amongst them
> But's stout as death, yet honest as the nature
> Of man first made, ere fraud and vice were fashions.

By the next day it is time for the poet to open his deluded hero's eyes. Jaffier's first shock, after he incautiously tells his wife about the plot to destroy Venice, is Belvidera's reaction. He had expected her to admire and praise him, but she does not take kindly to the prospect that her father is to be murdered by her husband, and all Venice laid waste. She protests to Jaffier (speaking, perhaps, as Otway's *raisonneur*),

> And canst thou shed the blood that gave me being?
> Nay, be a traitor too, and sell thy country?
> Can thy great heart descend so vilely low
> Mix with hired slaves, bravoes, and common stabbers,
> Nose-slitters, alley-lurking ruffians? Join
> With such a crew, and take a ruffian's wages,
> To cut the throats of wretches as they sleep?

With his heroic pose deflated, Jaffier is taken aback and confused. His second shock is Belvidera's revelation that during the past night old Renault crept to her bed and tried to ravish her. (The addition of "itching flesh" to Renault's character is necessary to show that the conspirators are not the high-minded patriots Jaffier thought them.) Shaken by the realization that he has trusted his wife and his honor to a villain, Jaffier complains,

> How cursed is my condition, tossed and jostled
> From every corner; Fortune's common fool,
> The jest of rogues, an instrumental ass,
> For villains to lay loads of shame upon,
> And drive about just for their ease and scorn!

Disturbed and doubtful, Jaffier meets with the conspirators for a final conference before the execution of the plot. Renault gives last-minute advice and bloody instructions. (Here Otway followed his source closely; once, for example, Renault called Pierre "Captain," a title used only by Saint-Reál.) Renault's murderous exhortation kindles Jaffier's imagination to a flame of horror. The other conspirators, including Pierre, listen with approval. At last Jaffier can stand it no longer; he slips out "in strange disorder," saying aside,

> O Belvidera, take me to your arms,
> And show me where's my peace, for I've lost it.

When we see him again, Belvidera is leading him to the Senate House. As she tells us later, she "chose the hour of love" to "bring him back to honor."

But now Jaffier is in a truly tragic dilemma. What is an honorable man to do when he finds that his own headlong passion and the persuasions of a trusted friend have betrayed him to evil? If he joins a Spanish plot to destroy Venice (analogous to a Communist plot to subvert the liberties of a nation), what is he to do when his eyes are opened? His conscience and reason tell him to disclose the plot — but he has sworn an oath, and he cannot bring himself to break his word and betray his friends. So it is with Jaffier. Belvidera urges him to discover the plot, save Venice, and gain immortal honor. She reminds him of Renault's attempt on her virtue, and paints in vivid images the prospective slaughter of reverend nobles, tender infants, and distracted mothers. In the horror of the bloody night to come, she argues, Renault might safely accomplish his planned rape upon her, and even lay a train for Jaffier's life. Love, the honor of a husband, and human compassion are all on Belvidera's side. Yet if Jaffier reveals the plot he will betray his oath and his "virtue, constancy, and friends" — especially his friend Pierre, who helped him in his hour of need. The beam of the balance trembles, but no matter which scale he chooses, Jaffier is doomed to destruction. Love and Belvidera outweigh honor and Pierre, and Jaffier makes his fatal decision to disclose the plot to the Venetian Senate, crying "Now the lot's cast, and, Fate, do what thou wilt."

In the last two acts the plot breaks down in a welter of confusions. Jaffier stands before the Duke of Venice and the hastily assembled Council of Ten (with a list of the conspirators in his hand) and demands full pardon for himself and the "lives of two and twenty friends" as the price for laying bare the conspiracy. The Council swears to grant his conditions. The conspirators are captured, offered a choice — "Pardon or death?" — and inexplicably all choose honorable death. Instead, the faithless Senators (for no apparent reason except that again Otway was following his source closely) decree shameful death by torture on the rack and the wheel. Pierre curses and strikes Jaffier and returns the dagger given with Belvidera as a pledge for his faith.

Now Jaffier is agonized by another tragic dilemma. Shall he try to retrieve his lost honor by slaying Belvidera — and so lose his love? Otway's fluid, emotional verse swells to new heights of passion. We are moved to pity for unfortunate Belvidera, the victim of her father's cruelty and her husband's folly, and to terror at the sight of half-mad Jaffier, tortured by his guilty fancies and fiddling with the hostage dagger in his bosom while he works himself into a murderous rage against his wife:

Where's my friend? my friend, thou smiling mischief?
Nay, shrink not, now 'tis too late. Thou shouldst have fled
When thy guilt first had cause, for dire revenge
Is up and raging for my friend. He groans —
Hark, how he groans! His screams are in my ears
Already; see, th' have fixed him on the wheel,
And now they tear him. — Murder! perjured Senate!
Murder! Oh! — Hark thee, trait'ress, thou hast done this;
Thanks to thy tears and false persuading love. —
How her eyes speak! — O thou bewitching creature!
Fumbling for his dagger.
Madness cannot hurt thee. Come, thou little trembler,
Creep, even into my heart, and there lie safe;
'Tis thy own citadel. — Hah! Yet stand off!
Heaven must have justice, and my broken vows
Will sink me else beneath its reaching mercy. —
I'll wink, and then 'tis done.

Love conquers again, and Belvidera lives — for a few more hours. At last Jaffier finds a solution to his problem and uses his dagger bravely, giving honorable death to Pierre, who is about to be broken on the wheel, and saving some of his own honor by suicide. The final episodes run riot with madness, ghosts, and horror, while a melancholy passing-bell tolls behind the scenes.

Venice is preserved — but who cares about Venice? Otway focuses all our emotions on Jaffier and Belvidera, changing his plot and characters to suit his tragic vision. Jaffier, an admirable protagonist, is destroyed by his own passions and the circumstances in which he is placed. Having free will, he is responsible for his decisions; he cannot blame Pierre, who is only half a villain.

But the "moral" of the play is not political. Although Otway was a sturdy Tory, he was not engaged in proving merely that any plot against an established state is evil, and that the good man who is caught on the wrong side is doomed to defeat. He calls our attention, rather, to what happens when two naive lovers are caught between the fell, incensèd points of mighty opposites: the mercenary revolutionists, and the cruel, oligarchic senate. Their destruction is terrifyingly inevitable, and their sufferings are pathetic.

Venice Preserved was a great success. Unfortunately, Otway wrote the play at a time when party feelings ran high, when the Whig attempt to replace James, Duke of York, with the bastard Duke of Monmouth as heir presumptive to the English throne loomed large in people's minds, and when every audience interpreted serious plays in terms of its own politics. Whatever Otway's intentions may have been, there is no doubt that the Whigs and Tories in the audience read contemporary political motifs into the play. Tradition has it, for example, that "when Leigh [Antonio] and Mrs. Currer [Acquilina] performed the parts of doting cully and rampant courtesan, the applause was as loud as the triumphant Tories, for so they were at that time, could bestow."

Otway himself added to the general confusion by an ambiguous prologue which fed fuel to partisan fires. Although he disclaimed any topical reference, he seemed to hint that there was a parallel between the leader of the Whigs, aging Anthony Ashley Cooper, Earl of Shaftesbury (whose enemies accused him of inordinate lechery), and Renault, the titular leader of the Venetian plot, a traitor who was

> very old,
> Turbulent, subtle, mischievous, and bold,
> Bloody, revengeful, and to crown his part,
> Loves fumbling with a wench with all his heart.

Then there was also Otway's obscenely comic Antonio, who seemed to have his local and personal application:

> Next is a senator that keeps a whore;
> In Venice none a higher office bore;
> To lewdness every night the lecher ran —

Show me, all London, such another man;
Match him at Mother Cresswold's if you can.
O Poland, Poland! had it been thy lot
T' have heard in time of this Venetian plot,
Thou surely chosen hadst one king from thence,
And honored them as thou hast England since.

Adding up these passages, and remembering that Shaftesbury was said to have aspired to the elective crown of Poland, most modern readers have concluded that Otway designed Renault to represent Shaftsbury in his secret capacity as the leader of the Whig conspiracy, and Antonio to represent him in his public function as a Member of the House of Lords. Further arguments for Antonio as a caricature of Shaftesbury are these: he is fond of public speaking; he sings a Whig song and addresses his mistress, Acquilina, as his "Tory, rory strumpet"; he is sixty-one years old, just about Shaftesbury's age; and his name suggests Shaftesbury's first name, Anthony.

These are good arguments; but we must note that Bedamar, not Renault, is the real leader of the plot against Venice; that Antonio is a common Italian name; that the first name of Leigh, the comedian who created the role of Antonio, was also Anthony; and that very few people knew or cared how old Shaftesbury was. Curiously, the best evidence for Renault and Antonio as satires on Shaftesbury appears in the prologue. Yet Restoration prologues, taken by themselves, are easily misinterpreted. Ordinarily a prologue was written just before the play's first performance. It was loaded with topical references, smart remarks, sneers at politicians, beaux, fops, critics, cuckolds, Whigs, Catholics, and what-not — all designed to make an audience sit up and take notice. If we ignore the prologue we find that the plot against Venice, although it bears a faint likeness to the Gunpowder Plot of 1605 or the Popish Plot of 1678, is not in the least like the Whig political conspiracy of 1679–1681 to force through Parliament a bill excluding the Duke of York from the succession to the throne. Attempts to interpret the play as a complete political satire result only in confusion, and any parallels drawn between the condition of Venice in 1618 and that of England in 1682 are likely to be misleading. Our only information about the state of Venice comes from Otway's conspirators, who are surely prejudiced reporters.

The resemblance between Renault and Shaftesbury is, at most, accidental. Otway took Renault bodily from Saint-Réal's narrative, adding only "itching flesh" to his character. The argument that Antonio, an invented character who has no plot function, was designed as a portrait of Shaftesbury — a thin, pale-faced little man, who carried a silver tap in his side to relieve a suppurating ulcer — rests in part on a misreading of the prologue. The English parallel for a Venetian senator would not be a Member of Parliament but an alderman of London — "Show me, all London, such another man." Although the allusion to Poland reminds us of the stale Tory joke that in 1674 Shaftesbury had hoped to be elected King of Poland, by 1682 the joke had become extensible to any ambitious Whig. Three months after *Venice Preserved,* Aphra Behn produced a farce, *The City Heiress,* in which Sir Timothy Treat-all, an unreconstructed Whig merchant, is gulled into thinking that he can be elected King of Poland. I suggest that in creating Antonio, Otway had a double purpose in mind: to provide a low-comedy satiric role for the popular actor Anthony Leigh, and to develop a bawdy subplot in contrast to the true-love theme of the main plot.

Leigh was a big, fat, round-faced comedian, famed for dialects and "patter" speeches — the voluble flow of foolish, repetitious talk which distinguishes Antonio from everyone else in the play. On his first appearance, Antonio greets Acquilina with:

> Nacky, Nacky, Nacky — how dost do, Nacky? Hurry durry. I am come, little Nacky; past eleven a-clock, a late hour; time in all conscience to go to bed, Nacky — Nacky, did I say? Aye, Nacky; Acquilina, lina, lina, quilina, quilina,

quilina, Acquilina, Nacquilina, Naquilina, Acky, Acky, Nacky, Nacky, queen Nacky — come, let's to bed — you fubbs, you pugg, you — you little puss — purree tuzzey — I am a senator.

ACQUILINA. You are a fool, I am sure.

ANTONIO. May be so, too, sweetheart. Never the worse senator for all that. Come, Nacky, Nacky, let's have a game at rump, Nacky.

Leigh was famous also for his portrayals of bestial, lecherous old men — especially City knights and aldermen. By 1682 the Whig party was so strong in the City that on the comic stage every City knight and alderman became, almost automatically, a satire on Whiggery. Antonio is a plump, well-fed senator, who is old, rich, powerful, impertinent, lecherous, cowardly, and clearly a Whig. To the dominantly Tory audience of *Venice Preserved* he must have been immediately recognizable as a typical caricature of a London alderman.

Although the scenes between Antonio (a masochist) and Acquilina are undoubtedly offensive — so offensive that eighteenth-century actors deleted them — they do not constitute an artistic blemish. They add to the malodor of sex which permeates the play. Pierre tells us that when he found Antonio in Acquilina's arms, he drove "the rank old bearded Hirco home." Antonio's slimy touch has so befouled Acquilina that when she begs Pierre to spend a night with her he refuses, saying, "No, there's fool, there's fool about thee." The stench of sex is noisome in the "Nicky-Nacky" scenes. When Antonio pretends to be a dog, Acquilina agrees to play, saying, "But let me beg your dogship to play your tricks over as fast as you can, that you may come to stinking the sooner and can be turned out of doors as you deserve." The stench is rank in Renault; as Jaffier tells Pierre the story of Renault's attempt on Belvidera, he says,

Oh, how the old fox stunk, I warrant thee,
When the rank fit was on him.

Against this mephitic background the love of Jaffier and Belvidera is sweet and clean. Yet it is frankly sensual, a passionate physical attachment. Belvidera's limbs, says Jaffier, are "framed for the tender offices of love," and he longs for her embraces. Belvidera would be alone with Jaffier, even in a desert, so that she could throw her arms about him and "give loose to love with kisses, kindling joys." When Jaffier threatens to kill her, Belvidera reminds him of their many nights of love,

> When our stringed hearts leaped to meet each other,
> And melting kisses sealed our lips together,
> When joys have left me gasping in thy arms.

This is frank, honest, conjugal love, limned boldly against a background of lechery, depravity, and perversion. The contrast serves to elevate the protagonists: two admirable people who wanted only to be left alone with their all-absorbing love, and who were destroyed by their own passions when their needs forced them into a harsh, pitiless world.

Whatever its structural faults, *Venice Preserved* touched every heart. Even John Dryden, an envious poet, paid his tribute to Otway for his greatest play. "I will not defend everything in his *Venice Preserved*," said Dryden, "but I must bear this testimony to his memory, that the passions are truly touched in it, though perhaps there is somewhat to be desired both in the grounds of them and in the height and elegance of expression; but Nature is there, which is the greatest beauty."

*** 10 ***

Pathetic Tragedy

IT IS NOT ALWAYS EASY to distinguish between high and pathetic tragedy. Usually pathetic tragedy — aesthetically a lower form, a "tear-jerker" — results from the deliberate attempt of a playwright to win pity for innocent, long-suffering victims of villainy, chance, or fate, or for sinners whose punishment is far out of proportion to their sins. An honest plea for pity is not to be scorned. Man needs to be reminded that pity for the unfortunate is a noble emotion, especially if it is designed to move an audience to remedial action. But lesser artists often present a picture of misfortune so falsified and overdrawn that pathos becomes bathos. Instead of an appeal to pity founded on a moral or social purpose, we have a deliberate pandering to the self-indulgence of tears. One must always be suspicious of pathetic tragedy.

Sometimes pathetic tragedy results from the playwright's failure to make his protagonist sufficiently admirable. No matter how many rocks the poet throws at the tragic character, the spectator can feel only pity, never the terror which comes from watching the inexorable destruction of greatness. More often pathetic tragedy results from weaknesses in plot and motivation.

The catastrophe, which is otherwise not inevitable, not grounded in character, hinges upon misunderstandings or mistakes, and the play is dominated more by circumstances than by the passions of the protagonist.

Thomas Otway's *The Orphan* (1680) is an excellent example of a pathetic tragedy which hinges upon mistakes. The scene is Bohemia, the country house of noble Acasto, who has retired from public affairs and brought his family to live in vernal privacy. The story of his two sons, twins who are rivals for the love of orphaned Monimia, Acasto's ward, had the potentialities of high tragedy, but Otway, who loved to dwell upon the misfortunes of lovers, turned it into a tragedy of tears. There are fatal weaknesses in character and motivation. Otway does his best to make the two brothers, Polydore and Castalio, admirable. We learn that

> They're both of nature mild, and full of sweetness.
> They came twins from the womb, and still they live
> As if they would go twins too to the grave.
> Neither has anything he calls his own,
> But of each other's joys as griefs partaking;
> So very honestly, so well they love,
> As they were only for each other born.

But now Monimia has matured to womanhood, with beauty

> that might shake the leagues
> Of mighty kings, and set the world at odds.

Each brother desires her, but each, claiming eagerness to go out into the wide world of war and politics, denies any intention of marrying her. Talking the matter over, they agree never to quarrel, no matter who wins and enjoys her. Polydore does his best to seduce Monimia, and when she rebuffs him he growls that he will bide his time and ravish her.

But Castalio, who truly loves Monimia, marries her, and, for reasons which are almost incredible, does so in secret. Then, again without plausible reason, he fails to tell his brother what he has done. Polydore, who rather to our surprise turns out to be an experienced wencher, overhears his brother making an assignation with Monimia, assumes that the appointment is for an illicit purpose, anticipates Castalio at the hour appointed, and revels all night in Monimia's charms, while poor Castalio, locked out on his nuptial night, wails at the moon. In short, for the sake of his plot, Otway makes Polydore a cad and Castalio a very silly fellow.

When the cheat is revealed, poor, deceived Monimia swoons, recovers, and rants,

> Let mischiefs multiply! Let every hour
> Of my loathed life yield me increase of horror!
> Oh, let the sun to these unhappy eyes
> Ne'er shine again, but be eclipsed for ever;
> May everything I look on seem a prodigy
> To fill my soul with terrors, till I quite
> Forget I ever had humanity,
> And grow a curser of the works of nature!

According to the conventions of seventeenth-century tragedy, the stain of incest, like that of adultery, is indelible, and dishonored Monimia can never be a wife to Castalio. She can only weep, wail, and complain against the fates.

The horrid sin is committed in the third act; the last two acts are filled with agonies, pressed down and running over. When Monimia finally makes Polydore understand that he has enjoyed his brother's wife, Polydore declaims,

> Let's find some place where adders nest in winter,
> Loathsome and venomous; where poisons hang
> Like gums against the walls; where witches meet
> By night, and feed upon some pampered imp,
> Fat with the blood of babes. There we'll inhabit
> And live up to the height of desperation.

> Desire shall languish like a withering flower,
> And no distinction of the sex be thought of.

But on second thought he decides to die. He provokes his brother to a duel, impales himself on Castalio's sword, and cries, dying,

> Blame not the heavens; here lies thy fate, Castalio.
> They're not the gods; 'tis Polydore has wronged thee.
> I've stained thy bed; thy spotless marriage joys
> Have been polluted by thy brother's lust.

Monimia wanders in, bemoans her hard lot, and dies of self-administered poison. Urged by his father to have patience, Castalio, whose tears are drowning the stage, cries,

> Patience! Preach it to the winds,
> The roaring seas or raging fires! The knaves
> That teach it laugh at ye when ye believe them.
> Strip me of all the common needs of life,
> Scald me with leprosy, let friends forsake me,
> I'll bear it all; but, cursed to the degree
> That I am now, 'tis this must give me patience.
> Thus I find rest and shall complain no more.
> *Stabs himself.*
> Now all I beg is, lay me in one grave
> Thus with my love. Farewell! I now am — nothing.
> *Dies.*

There is hardly a dry eye in the house; even the players weep. According to Betterton, Mrs. Barry, as Monimia, "never spoke these words in *The Orphan,* 'Ah, poor Castalio' [V, ii], without weeping." Although there is no perceptible moral, except that "the fates have plagued us," and the play is full of bombast and rant, it was immensely successful and remained a stock tragedy throughout the eighteenth century — perhaps because Otway's emotional language concealed its dramatic faults.

The weakness of tragedy based on a fatal accident or mistake is further illustrated by Dryden's *Don Sebastian* (1689). The setting is Barbary. Sebastian, captive King of Portugal, loves and secretly marries Almeyda, a Barbary princess. After much villainy, plotting, poisoning, and the murder of Muley-Moloch, the tyrannical King of Barbary, who had sought to ravish Almeyda, the villains are all defeated, and it seems that the lovers will be able to live happily ever after. Suddenly the happy ending is reversed; an old courtier reveals that Almeyda is Sebastian's half-sister, the fruit of his father's adulterous love for Zayda, exiled Queen of Barbary. The crime of incest, even though it was committed unknowingly, should have been expiated in blood, but Dryden was kinder than Otway. As he explained in his preface to the play (printed in 1690), death would not be consonant with poetic justice — "an involuntary sin deserves not death." Instead the play ends with an appeal to pity for the unfortunate lovers. Sebastian decides to retire to a hermitage, and Almeyda to enter a nunnery. As they part, Almeyda moans,

> Now I would speak the last farewell, I cannot.
> It would be still farewell a thousand times;
> And, multiplied in echoes, still farewell.
> I will not speak, but think a thousand thousand.
> And be thou silent too, my lost Sebastian;
> So let us part in the dumb pomp of grief.
> My heart's too great, or I would die this moment;
> But death, I thank him, in an hour has made
> A mighty journey, and I haste to meet him.
> *She staggers, and her women hold her up.*
> SEBASTIAN. Help to support this feeble drooping flower,
> This tender sweet, so shaken by the storm;
> For these fond arms must thus be stretched in vain.
> And never, never must embrace her more.
> 'Tis past — my soul goes in that word farewell.

It is all very sad; but perhaps the saddest fact is that, by a trick, Dryden turned a rousing villain melodrama into a pathetic tragedy. The moral of the play seems to be (as Moses discovered on Mount Sinai)

> That unrepented crimes of parents dead,
> Are justly punished on their children's head.

Gradually, as the century wore towards its close and the respectable middle classes drifted into the theaters, the emphasis in pathetic tragedy shifted towards the misfortunes of womanhood. At the beginning of the Restoration era, the audiences were predominantly male, and drama exalted male virtues. But the women, especially the untitled ladies of the Town and City, were increasingly resentful of their underprivileged status and of the masculine delusion that they were created for man's pleasure and to bear his children. The dramatists sought to please the ladies by dwelling more upon man's perfidy, woman's virtue, and the sad plight of distressed damsels, ravished virgins, and melancholy wives.

Although Thomas Southerne's *The Fatal Marriage, or The Innocent Adultery* (1694) is blemished by a farcical subplot, it is still a good example of the pathetic tragedy which concentrates upon the quandary of a woeful wife. It was very popular in its own day, and in 1757 Garrick gave it a new lease on life by removing the comic plot and renaming it *Isabella, or The Fatal Marriage.* The apparent moral of the play was stated by old Count Baldwin:

> To erring youth there's some compassion due;
> But while with rigor you their crimes pursue,
> What's their misfortune is a crime in you.
> Hence learn, offending children to forgive;
> Leave punishment to Heaven, 'tis Heaven's prerogative.

But perhaps the real moral is Isabella's mad cry,

> I did not hope to find
> Justice on earth; 'tis not in Heaven neither.

The scene is Brussels, the time about 1676. The erring youth is Count Baldwin's elder son, Biron, who secretly married Isabella, an apostate nun. Biron's angry father disinherited him and somehow forced him to go to the siege of Candy, where he presumably lost his life. (Southerne admitted that he took the hint for his play from Aphra Behn's novel, *The History of the Nun, or The Fair Vow-breaker,* and that he wrote the character of Isabella with the great tragedienne Elizabeth Barry in mind.)

As the play opens, Isabella has been a widow for nearly seven years. She has supported herself and her son by pawning her jewels, but she is deeply in debt. She makes a last appeal to Count Baldwin, who drives her away with curses. Her creditors descend upon her in a body. Villeroy, a wealthy, honorable gentleman, who has besieged her steadily with offers of marriage, pays her debts, and in a burst of gratitude she marries him. The next day Villeroy has to go off on a short journey, and that night Biron returns.

It seems that all this time he has been a slave to the Turks. He had written often, but (as we learn later) his wicked younger brother, Carlos, who wanted to be Count Baldwin's heir, had intercepted the letters. As a second line of defense against Biron's possible return, Carlos had encouraged Isabella to marry Villeroy.

When Isabella recognizes Biron she faints in his arms, recovers, and gives way to joy:

> 'Tis he himself, my Biron, the dear man!
> My true loved husband! do I hold you fast,
> Never to part again? Can I believe it?
> Nothing but you could work so great a change.
> There's more than life itself in dying here;
> If I must fall, 'tis welcome in these arms.

The first ecstasy is followed by a babble of questions; then she remembers that she has married Villeroy, and grief stabs through her happiness. She cannot bring herself to tell Biron. She temporizes and carries on a long internal debate until her conflicting emotions drive her to the edge of madness. Innocently she has committed adultery and bigamy. If Biron had returned a few days later, after the expiration of seven full years, the law would have excused the bigamy. But Isabella cares only about her broken vows of love and chastity. As she prepares unwillingly to follow Biron to bed, she is torn and distracted:

> Biron, my husband —
> To follow him to bed — my husband! ha!
> What then is Villeroy? but yesterday
> That very bed received him for its lord —
> Yet a warm witness of my broken vows —
> To send another to usurp his room!
> O Biron! hadst thou come but one day sooner,
> I would have followed thee through beggary,
> Through all the chances of this weary life,
> Wandered the many ways of wretchedness
> With thee, to find a hospitable grave;
> For that's the only bed that's left me now.
> *Weeping.*
> What's to be done?

What, indeed? Except by her death, how can Isabella expiate her sin? A modern spectator might well agree with Dryden, that "an involuntary sin deserves not death," but Southerne seems to have had in mind the Biblical injunction, "If a man be found lying with a woman married to an husband, then they shall both of them die," which left no loophole for accidents. English law and custom had taken off the death penalty for adultery, but not the shame for a woman caught *in flagrante*. Since conventional morality threw all the onus on the erring wife, Southerne has Isabella in the jaws of a vise. She has two living husbands, and she has been "by both enjoyed." Clearly she has committed adultery with Villeroy and must pay the penalty.

Later that night, Biron learns from Isabella's servants the full story of her woes and her second marriage. He decides heroically that only his own death can save her from ruin. But before he can work out a suicide plan, his brother, Carlos, who has miraculously learned of his return, calls him to the door, attacks him with a band of bravoes, and gives him his death wound. Villeroy, returning opportunely, drives off the villains and captures one of them.

Now the stage fills. Biron dies, after "a long farewell, and a last, parting kiss." Isabella, now completely mad, throws herself beside his body. Carlos and Count Baldwin appear, to accuse Villeroy of Biron's murder. But the captured bravo has been racked until he confesses all — evidently a rack was standard equipment for a Brussels household. Carlos admits his villainy and is turned over to the law. Isabella raves, stabs herself, and dies. Villeroy mourns, and Count Baldwin, promising to be a tender parent to his orphaned grandson, blames his own "flinty heart" for everything.

The Fatal Marriage has all the ingredients of pathetic tragedy: a cynical villain who overreaches himself; a hard-hearted father, a helpless infant, a lost and despairing husband, a pitiable wife who has wept steadily for seven years, madness, suicide, murder, and an all-pervading melancholy gloom. This is the stuff of sentimental drama; it lacks only the reformation of the villain. The play has neither social nor moral purpose; it is neither a plea for injured womanhood nor a protest against the double standard of morality. Southerne refuses to consider any common-sense solution to Isabella's problem — an appeal, say, to the ecclesiastical courts for the annulment of her second marriage. Instead he keeps his victim isolated from reasonable counsellors and dwells upon her agonies to tear our heart-strings and move us to tears.

Isabella's long soliloquies, broken speeches, and flights of madness must have taxed even Elizabeth Barry's histrionic powers. Southerne paid the actress a handsome compliment: "I could not, if I would, conceal what I owe Mrs. Barry; and I should despair of ever being able to pay her, if I did not imagine that I have been a little accessary to the great applause that everybody gives her, in saying she outplays herself. . . . I made the play for her part, and her part has made the play for me."

The Fatal Marriage, plus such other pathetic tragedies as John Bankes's *Vertue Betrayed, or Anna Bullen* (1682), his *The Innocent Usurper* (1694), Granville's *Heroic Love* (1697), and Motteux' *Beauty in Distress* (1698) prepared the way for the "she-tragedy" of the eighteenth century, as it was developed by "soft, complaining" Rowe in *The Fair Penitent* (1703) and *Jane Shore* (1714). The age of sentiment and tears was ushered in with showers.

*** 11 ***

The Comic Sock

COMEDY was the Restoration's finest dramatic flower, yet few contemporary critics found occasion to admire its gaudy blossoms. They all agreed that, because the action of comedy was "trivial" and its persons traditionally of inferior rank, it was a lower form of art than tragedy, and appropriately written in prose instead of verse. Most of the critics argued that the function of comedy was to hold the mirror up to nature and depict the vices and follies of mankind in order to reform the age. Sir Richard Blackmore, in his preface to *Prince Arthur* (1695), insisted that the business of comedy was "to render vice ridiculous, to expose it to public derision and contempt, and to make men ashamed of vile and sordid actions." A nonjuring clergyman, Jeremy Collier, in *A Short View of the Immorality and Profaneness of the English Stage* (1698), summed up fifty years of critical debate in a dogmatic statement: "The business of plays is to recommend virtue and discountenance vice; to show the uncertainty of human greatness, the sudden turns of fate, and the unhappy conclusions of violence and injustice; 'tis to expose the singularities of pride and fancy, to make folly and falsehood contemptible, and to bring everything that is ill under infamy and neglect. . . . The end of comedy [is] the exposing of knavery and making lewdness ridiculous."

The reader of Restoration comedy quickly discovers that, on the whole, it tends to recommend lewdness and is usually cynical about chastity; that it laughs at folly, rewards some kinds of knavery, and admires practically everything Collier thought of as evil. Yet the Restoration dramatists were cultivated, intelligent men, interested in the social, intellectual, and aesthetic problems of their generation. Like most of the people in their audiences, they were rational hedonists, but very few were rakes.

Of course the comic dramatists paid lip service to conventional morality, and, if pressed, would claim a reformatory purpose. Probably some of them were sincere. Richard Flecknoe, a priest turned poet, insisted in "A Short Treatise of the English Stage" (1664) that the stage should "render folly ridiculous, vice odious, and virtue and nobleness . . . amiable and lovely." His own comedies were decent enough but so dull that Dryden, in *Mac Flecknoe* (1682), represented their author as King of the realm of Nonsense.

Skipping forward half a century, we find George Farquhar, in *A Discourse upon Comedy* (1702), making the surprising statement that "the splenatic wit, the beau courtier, the heavy citizen, the fine lady and her fine footman, come all [to the theater] to be instructed." He tempered his remark with an argument which by his time had become a cliché, that "to make the moral instructive, you must make the play diverting." Farquhar's usual practice was to make his comedies diverting and to let instruction go hang. Thomas Shadwell argued steadily for comedy as moral instruction, with "virtue being exalted and vice depressed," yet some of his comedies are as lubricious as any written by his more sinful brethren. When Shadwell died in 1692, a writer in *The Gentleman's Journal* declared that his plays were as useful as they were diverting, and that by his comedies he had "shamed misers into liberality," made bullies tamer and prodigals wiser, and had reclaimed and reformed "hypocrites, coquettes, fops, gamesters . . . fools, and madmen." We have only his word for this.

Most Restoration poets would have agreed with Dryden, who, in his preface to *An Evening's Love* (printed in 1671), insisted that the chief end of comedy was "divertisement and delight," with instruction only remotely second, and denied the charge that he had rewarded "debauched persons" at the end of the comedy, thereby violating the principle of poetic justice. "The business of the [comic] poet," he said, "is to make you laugh. When he writes humor, he makes folly ridiculous; when wit, he moves you, if not always to laughter, yet to a pleasure that is more noble. And if he works a cure on folly and the small imperfections in mankind by exposing them to public view, that cure is not performed by an immediate operation. For it works first on the ill nature of the audience; they are moved to laugh by the representation of deformity; and the shame of that laughter teaches us to amend what is ridiculous in our manners." As for morality, Dryden denied that the principle of poetic justice applied to comedy, and that he himself sought "to make libertines amiable." In fact, he said, he married off his libertine heroes at the end of a comedy to reclaim them from vice, "for then, enjoying what they desire in one, they cease to pursue the love of many."

The last argument sounds suspiciously naive, but Dryden was always expert at rationalizing his practices. The fact is that, like his fellow poets, he gave his sophisticated audience what it demanded in comedy, including amiable libertines, emancipated young ladies, brisk dialogue, *double entendres,* and amusing, erotic scenes. But neither he nor his fellows thought their work licentious or obscene so long as they avoided bawdy, vulgar language.

It is true that in his *To the Pious Memory of . . . Mrs. Anne Killigrew* (1686) Dryden wrote what sounds like an abject apology for the licentiousness of some of his plays:

> O gracious God! How far have we
> Profaned thy heav'nly gift of poesy;
> Made prostitute and profligate the muse,
> Debased to each obscene and impious use,
> Whose harmony was first ordained above
> For tongues of angels and for hymns of love?
> O wretched we! why were we hurried down
> This lubrique and adult'rate age
> (Nay, added fat pollutions of our own)
> T' increase the steaming ordure of the stage?

The passage is appropriate to the high moral attitude of a poet writing an ode in praise of virgin virtue, but it should not be read as Dryden's repentance for his dramatic sins. A few years later he heaped the steaming ordures of the stage with a wickedly amusing comedy, *Amphitryon, or The Two Socias* (1690), in which Jupiter deftly cuckolds Amphitryon twice, and the dialogues between Mercury and Alcmena's beautiful slave, Phaedra, are saturated with sex.

It was not until Jeremy Collier made his famous attack against the stage in 1698 that Dryden, now old and weary, admitted that in some things Collier had taxed him justly. "I have pleaded guilty," he wrote in the preface to the *Fables* (1700), "to all thoughts and expressions of mine which can be truly argued of obscenity, profaneness, or immorality, and retract them." But by 1700 the Town, once a homogeneous blend of courtiers and private gentry, had become an oil-and-vinegar mixture of moral bourgeois and genteel sophisticates, with the moralists atop.

The "immorality" of Restoration comedy has been debated by generations of critics. Led by Macaulay, the moral Victorians condemned late seventeenth-century drama as profligate, vicious, and indecent. They could never forgive the comic writers their refusal to take sex seriously and their attempts to rationalize sex relationships. Macaulay said of Wycherley's comedies, "In truth Wycherley's indecency is protected against the critic as a skunk is protected against the hunters. It is safe, because it is too filthy to handle and too noisome to approach." On the other hand, Charles Lamb maintained that Restoration "artificial comedy" (or "comedy of manners") was amoral, that it dwelt in the land "of cuckoldry — the Utopia of gallantry, where pleasure is duty, and the manners perfect freedom. It is altogether a speculative scene of things, which has no reference whatever to the world that is." Lamb has been followed by generations of modern critics, who have emphasized the "artificiality" of Restoration comedy, while dwelling at length on its "manners," wit, and polish.

The positions of both Macaulay and Lamb (and their followers) are impossibly extreme. Restoration comedy exaggerates, of course, as all comedy must, but it is no more artificial than the comedy of any other age. It is neither amoral nor, in the context of its audience, immoral; and it seems indecent only to prudes repelled by the earthy language of the seventeenth century, often larded with Anglo-Saxon monosyllables. Restoration comedy developed its own moral code in keeping with the naturalistic bent of the Restoration coterie. It is immoral only in terms of the conventional Christian morality adhered to by those who mistake frankness for immorality, and never have any fun. It must be judged on its own terms.

The Restoration concept of laughter was based on the egoistic theory of the philosopher Hobbes, in *The Leviathan* (1651), that man is surprised into laughter because he feels suddenly superior to someone else. "Sudden glory," said Hobbes, "is the passion which maketh those grimaces called laughter; and is caused either by some sudden act of their own that pleaseth them, or by the apprehension of some deformed thing in another, by comparison whereof they suddenly applaud themselves." The Restoration comic spirit acknowledged only the rule of reason — "The world is a comedy to those that think, a tragedy to those that feel." Because conventional morality seemed unreasonable, the comic spirit was anti-moral. Its weapons were exaggeration, caricature, burlesque, parody, ridicule, vituperation, and satire — the product of indignation recollected in tranquillity.

To some extent all true comedy is at odds with conventional

morality. Morality demands an ordered world; at the same time it poses problems to which we have no answers. To avoid the problems, we turn to comedy, which brings confusion into the moral world, challenges its values, and sweeps its problems under the rug of laughter. Restoration comedy is more obviously anti-moral than the comedy of other periods because it was encouraged by a libertine Court and King — as Dryden wrote in 1700, "Whitehall the naked Venus first revealed" — and by a worldly-wise coterie of cynical aristocrats, who associated conventional morality with republicanism and Puritanism, and condemned it as canting hypocrisy.

At the beginning of the period, the theaters revived a mixed lot of Elizabethan, Jacobean, and Caroline comedies. The first new plays after 1660 were written by older craftsmen steeped in the traditions of the past: Davenant, Thomas and William Killigrew, Stapylton, Tuke, Porter, Robert Howard, Cowley, and Wilson. They turned out tragicomedies, pastorals, Spanish intrigue comedies, wooden romantic plays set in Cloud-Cuckoo-Land, gulling comedies, and humors plays in the Jonsonian tradition. Even Macaulay could hardly object to the morality of these early Restoration plays.

The new playwrights who soon dispossessed their older colleagues followed the English comic tradition but developed their craft in response to the changing demands of the new genteel audience. For instance, in 1663 John Dryden, one of the first of the young poets, produced *The Wild Gallant,* a poor, rough-and-tumble comedy which failed. Four years later he revised the play and brought it on the stage again. During those four years Dryden had learned a great deal about his audience, particularly about the once-banished Court, which,

> with lewdness fraught,
> The seeds of open vice returning brought.

Dryden had collaborated with Sir Robert Howard in writing a heroic play, *The Indian Queen;* he had produced a moderately successful romantic intrigue comedy, *The Rival Ladies;* another heroic play, *The Indian Emperor;* and a two-plot tragicomedy, *Secret Love, or The Maiden Queen.* He had noted the audience's preference for the more sophisticated comedies of Beaumont and Fletcher, and their delight in sparkling repartee, in satiric hits at conventional morality, and in the characters of witty libertines and brisk ladies — especially as personated by Charles Hart and "pretty, witty" Nell Gwyn. In his prologue for the revival of *The Wild Gallant,* Dryden apologized for his earlier version of the comedy:

> while knowledge he did want,
> Our unfledged author writ a *Wild Gallant.*
> He thought him monstrous lewd (I'll lay my life),
> Because suspected with his landlord's wife;
> But since his [the poet's] knowledge of the Town began,
> He thinks him now a very civil man,
> And, much ashamed of what he was before,
> Has fairly played him at three wenches more.
> 'Tis some amends his [the poet's] frailties to confess;
> Pray pardon him his want of wickedness.
> He's towardly, and will come on apace;
> His frank confession shows he has some grace.

Here "wickedness" is equivalent to roguishness, not to evil. Dryden had learned that his audience delighted in the mischievous, sportive tricks of young libertines, "whose faults and vices," he said indulgently, "are but the sallies of youth and the frailties of human nature."

Dryden's contemporaries discovered the taste of the new audience as he did, by trial and error. Thus James Howard's first play, *The English Monsieur* (1663), was an episodic intrigue comedy in the old coarse vein. He scored a hit with his second, *All Mistaken, or The Mad Couple* (1667), which made much of a pair of witty lovers; rakish Philidor, who has six mistresses yet falls in love with madcap Mirida, who already has two suitors, one fat and one lean. George Etherege's first comedy, *The Comical Revenge, or Love in a Tub* (1664), was a two-part play, with one part romance and the other a gulling comedy — "which is very merry," said Mr. Pepys, "but only so by gesture, not wit at all, which methinks is beneath the [Duke's] house." Etherege's second play, *She Would If She Could* (1668), was "roguish and witty," cynical, and anti-moral. The new poets quarried foreign comedy for characters and situations, but their products were still essentially English. "Our plots," said Dryden, "are weaved in English looms."

By 1668 the new mode was so well established that Shadwell, in his preface to *The Sullen Lovers,* complained, "In the plays which have been wrote of late, there is no such thing as perfect character, but the two chief persons are most commonly a swearing, drinking, whoring ruffian for a lover, and an impudent ill-bred tom-rig for a mistress, and these are the fine people of the play; and there is that latitude in this, that almost anything is proper for them to say; but their chief subject is bawdy and profaneness, which they call brisk writing." This was the new comedy, a blend of many native and a few foreign elements, the comedy which reflected the cynicism and hedonism of the coterie for which it was written. It was characterized by brisk dialogue, cynical and sexual wit, libertine gentlemen, and emancipated ladies.

It was characterized also by various unconventional attitudes which, in a very short time, became dramatic clichés. Consider, for example, the comic attitude toward marriage (especially the arranged marriage), which was conventionally regarded as a sacred and indissoluble union — a match made in Heaven. Anti-marriage quips are common enough in older English plays, but the Restoration poets developed the quips into full fledged themes and plots. They ridiculed marriage as at best a necessary evil, to be entered into only when the bride was both rich and beautiful and the groom needed an estate. By 1673, when Dryden wrote the comic scenes of *Marriage à la Mode,* the anti-marriage theme had become a fixed dramatic convention. Marriage was equated with damnation. Thus Palamede is courting Doralice, who tells him that she is married. "Art thou married?" he cries. "O thou damnable, virtuous woman." But he himself is to be married soon to a rich bride chosen by his father — "Married, past redemption." Doralice's husband, Rhodophil, tells his friend Palamede, "The greatest misfortune imaginable is fallen upon me. In one word, I am married, wretchedly married, and have been above these two years." Yet his wife is young, beautiful, gay, and witty; the only thing wrong with her is the name of "wife." He loved her, he submits, "a whole half year . . . but then the world began to laugh at me, and a certain shame of being out of fashion seized me."

With Palamede trying to cuckold Rhodophil, who at the same time is pursuing Palamede's bride-to-be, Melantha, the plot begins to look like an erotic merry-go-round, which could easily end in a *ménage à quatre.* But Dryden introduces a new incongruity: because Palamede finds Doralice attractive, Rhodophil falls in love with her again, and because Rhodophil finds Melantha attractive, Palamede decides to marry her. In effect, the comedy is a witty plea for the validity of married love.

In addition to playing with the anti-marriage theme, the Restoration comic poets rang the changes on a cluster of comic conventions, or clichés. For example: constant lovers and all husbands are dull. All women are wanton and must be carefully guarded against handsome young libertines. A lusty young woman married against her will to an old husband is sure to cuckold him. A young wife with an old husband needs neither wooing nor persuasion to commit adultery, merely an opportunity. Every young rakehell spends his waking hours in search of willing wenches. The rake who shares a bed with another man's wife does her a double favor — he satisfies her lust and helps her revenge herself on her unpleasant husband. Widows and elderly women are inordinately lustful. Old men are lecherous, sexually abnormal, or impotent.

Of course, very few people believed these dramatic myths or tried to live by them, but they are some of the commonplaces of Restoration comedy. The fact that cases illustrative of each cliché may appear in the pages of Restoration social history is beside the point. The comic poets did not (as they claimed) hold a mirror up to the fullness of nature. They did not try to create an illusion of average normal human — or even coterie — experience. Instead, like good journalists, they selected from contemporary life those characters, speeches, and situations which they knew would amuse their audiences. In his epilogue to *Ibrahim* (1676), a heroic play, Elkanah Settle protested to his audience,

> There's ne'er a comic writer but will say
> You're all of you the patterns of his play;
> Yet takes your pictures at so damned a light,
> Paints you so ugly that your looks would fright;
> And yet their plays are your most dear delight.
> Why in your hearts may not the heroics share?
> Those make you worse, these better than you are.

The new comedy was not completely free from restraints. There were always those in the audience who, like Shadwell, objected to plain dealing as debauchery and to plain speaking as obscenity, and there were others who argued for decorum on neoclassic grounds. Although comedy could laugh at parsons and chaplains, it dared not attack the hierarchy of the established church. Of course it could not jest with royalty or true nobility; the occasional lord ridiculed in comedy is usually an upstart who has bought his title. When comedy ventured into politics it was limited to jeering at levelers, republicans, and Whigs; after 1689 it could laugh only at nonjurors and Jacobites. The well-nigh universal aristocratic practice of keeping mistresses was not a safe subject for satire, as Dryden found to his cost with the suppression of *The Kind Keeper*. Taboo also were God, motherhood, and the flag.

Nevertheless, once the new mode was well established, the Restoration comic spirit, released from most conventional restraints, was free to turn loose its brutal weapons against fops, fools, bullies, braggarts, country bumpkins, sharpers, hypocrites, social climbers, jealous husbands, cuckolds, heavy fathers, lecherous old men and women, fanatics, foreigners, citizens, and aldermen. It laughed at senseless rules and repressive institutions; stuck pins in stuffed shirts; dragged skeletons from closets; exploded myths; and showed the cloven hoof beneath the godly robe. It laughed coarsely at venereal disease ("the pox"), at mistaken marriages, and lost maidenheads. It made good-natured fun of pimps, bawds, and whores, not because they were immoral, but because in a reasonable world they were ridiculous. Chuckling quietly, it presented a sex intrigue — the efforts of a "whoring ruffian" to bed an "impudent tom-rig" without benefit of clergy — as an amusing sport which gave pleasure to both the hunter and the quarry. It presented libertines and Truewits to be admired, and moralists and would-be wits to be laughed at as contemptible and ridiculous. It ran the gamut from broad, vulgar farce, through burlesque and intrigue comedy, humors and satiric comedy, to the comedy of wit. At the close of the century, it turned, like a penitent prodigal, to the comedy of tears.

*** 12 ***

Farce, Burlesque, and Intrigue

MOST COMEDY arises from the incongruity or contrast between the normal and the abnormal, the commonplace and the exaggerated, or the expected and the unexpected. Physical incongruity is the lowest, most obvious, and most popular form of comedy. An audience made up of normal, conventionally dressed people laughs at oddities of feature, form, and dress — an overlarge mouth, an overlong nose, a fat man, a thin man, a crooked man, or someone in eccentric, fantastic, or epicene dress. (Curiously, a woman in man's clothes is attractive; a man in woman's clothes is ridiculous.) Of course, extreme oddities are not amusing; Bardolph's red nose is comic, but Cyrano de Bergerac's long nose is pathetic.

Physical comedy depends further upon the degradation resulting from "prat-falls," beatings, and assaults with such harmless weapons as slapsticks and custard pies. The physical humiliation of a comic character arouses the cruel laughter of superiority. The greater the contrast, the louder the laughter. The fall of a cripple brings murmurs of sympathy; but the fall of a pompous gentleman in frock coat and silk hat, "barbered and upholstered at incredible cost" (to borrow Mark Twain's phrase), arouses the loud laughter of the proletariat.

The typical Restoration playgoer, unlike his modern counterpart (let us hope), was as childishly quick to laugh at physical deformities or uncouth behavior as a mere citizen or yokel. Londoners of every degree went to Bartholomew or Southwark fair to be amused by the antics of "Jack Pudding" clowns, fantastic mountebanks, merry-andrews, scaramouches, rope-dancers, and puppets — or paid a penny for admission to Bethlehem Hospital for the insane, to giggle at the grotesqueries of the Bedlamites. In the theaters, Restoration audiences laughed at a lover caught in his mistress's closet, a dignified gentleman minus his breeches, a zany bedaubed with mud, a cheating servant belabored with a padded club, or a cowardly bully kicked and cuffed. The protoype of the modern custard pie was the cup custard of a Jack Pudding or a homely sack posset — hot milk curdled with wine. Mr. Pepys described the comedy of Davenant's *The Man's the Master* (1668) as "sorry, poor stuff, of eating of sack posset, and beslabbering themselves, and mirth fit for clowns."

The comedy of cuckoldry, too, was, by implication, physical mirth and fit for clowns. In the world of make-believe, the husband whose wife was unfaithful was usually presented as a comic figure, to be laughed at for his jealousy, his stupidity, or his credulity. In reality, the seventeenth-century cuckold was a pitiable fellow. He could sue in the ecclesiastical courts for a divorce "from bed and board," but he could get a true divorce with permission to marry again only through a bill approved by the House of Lords. To get any measure of legal relief he had to parade his shame in public and endure the cynical laughter of those who, knowing (or believing) that their own wives were chaste, enjoyed their superiority to the poor cuckold. The traditional symbol of the cuckold was a pair of horns, branched like a deer's; the derisive gesture was a fist, held up with two fingers straight. There was no equivalent symbol for the wife of an unfaithful husband.

Some physical comedy is likely to appear in any kind of comic drama, even in the comedy of wit. Farce is dominantly physical comedy. It deals in absurd and exaggerated situations, implausible complications, cheatings, cuckoldry, slapstick, and horseplay. Burlesque is farce which reduces a higher, or more serious, kind of drama to the lowest possible terms. Intrigue comedy, closely related to farce, lacks the roughness of slapstick and places more emphasis upon the ingenious manipulation of characters, situations, disguises, and misunderstandings in one or more sex intrigues, which usually end in marriage.

The Restoration poets professed to despise farce, a low form of comedy which, with some justice, they believed to be imported from France. In *A Parallel betwixt Poetry and Painting* (1695) Dryden, who had a definition for everything, wrote, "A farce is that in poetry, which *grotesque* is in a picture. The persons and action of a farce are all unnatural, and the manners false, inconsisting with the characters of mankind." Starting from much the same premises, Nahum Tate, in his preface to *A Duke and No Duke* (printed in 1685), argued that it was hard to write good farce because "tragedy, comedy, and pastoral itself subsist upon Nature; so that whoever has a genius to copy her is assured of success, and all the world affords him subjects; whereas the business of farce is to exceed Nature and probability. But then there are so few improbabilities that will appear pleasant, and so much nicety required in the management, that the performance will be found extremely difficult." Perhaps his contention explains why dramatic poets in all ages have produced so many bad farces.

It was generally agreed that refined people detested farce, and that only the coarse-minded enjoyed it. Thus, in his prologue to *The Old Troop* (ca. 1663), a rough farce, John Lacy appealed to the easy-going galleries, as opposed to the critical pit:

> To you that judges are in th' public street
> Of ballad without sense or even feet;

To you that laugh aloud with wide-mouthed grace
To see Jack Pudding's custard thrown in 's face,
To you I do address; for you I write;
From you I hope protection here tonight.

Nevertheless, in 1671, as Dryden admitted in the preface to *An Evening's Love,* farces were "the most frequent entertainment of the stage." The taste for farce, even with refined auditors, grew steadily as the century wore on. In his dedication to *Greenwich Park* (1691) William Mountfort complained that "we can see the Town throng to a farce, and Hamlet not bring charges [pay the costs of production]." A year later, Dryden, in the preface to *Cleomenes,* deplored the fact that "the world is running mad after farce, the extremity of bad poetry." Some of Dryden's own comedies are perilously close to farce, and *The Kind Keeper* (1678) is a good example of the genre.

Of the many farcical situations used in Restoration comedy, here are a few samples chosen at random. A rake seeking "the favor" from a citizen's young wife is caught in her bedroom by the unexpected return of her husband and has to hide in a closet, under the bed, or behind the bed-curtains. To conceal his identity, an amorous rake has to endure insults, blows, and degradation. An old man, fobbed off with an ancient governess in place of a young beauty, identifies her by her lack of teeth. A rake, tricked by his sweetheart, is bound to a couch and beaten. A man dresses as a woman to get access to his mistress, and is beaten. A foolish old citizen is made to look ridiculous when tricksters dressed as Turks create him a Turkish dignitary — a "Mamamouchi." A country squire is initiated into the noble order of asses by tricksters who throw bumpers of wine in his face as he kneels before them. Two fools, sought by the watch, pose as figures in a tapestry; the watchmen drink wine and throw the lees in their faces. A jilting wench gets a fool's clothes and money and, as he is about to climb into her bed, springs a trap which drops him into a sewer — "a common shore." As a rake is climbing a ladder to a lady's window, a "Maid within shoots a squirt of blood in 's face and lets off a pistol." A rake gambles with a greedy citizen and wins a night of love with his wife. The citizen has to act as pander and hold the door. Enough!

The label "farce" is not in itself derogatory; there are good farces and bad. For example, seen in terms of its purpose and its theatrical effects, Edward Ravenscroft's *The London Cuckolds* (November, 1681) is a good farce. At least it is an excellent example of Restoration farce. It deals in physical incongruity and humiliation, absurd and exaggerated situations, cuckoldry, slapstick, and horseplay. Although its situations are clichés, the poet rang some ingenious changes upon them. The stock characters, subordinated to the plot, are sufficiently individualized to come to life upon the stage.

Ravenscroft's cuckolds are three rich, elderly citizens: Alderman Doodle, Scrivener Dashwell, and Alderman Wiseacre. As citizens they would be fair game for farce at any time, but in November, 1681, they were "petitioning" citizens, that is, Whigs who, after the dissolution of Parliament on March 28, 1681, petitioned for the election of a new Parliament. "A petitioner!" cries one rakehell to another; "Cuckold the rogue for that very reason."

Doodle is married to a lustful young wife, Arabella, a wit; Dashwell to a lustful young wife, Eugenia, who pretends piety; and in the course of the comedy, Wiseacre (who is "near fifty") marries Peggy, a remarkably ignorant country girl just fourteen years old. Obviously none of the women loves her mate. Mrs. Dashwell and Mrs. Doodle are gentlewomen, compelled by their families to marry wealthy citizens.

The problem proposed by the farce is this: is a husband's honor safer in the hands of a witty wife, a "pious" wife, or an ignorant wife? The three libertines who help provide the answer are Loveday, formerly a suitor to "godly" Mrs. Dashwell; hardworking Ramble, a very unlucky fellow; and easy-going Townly, who catches the birds after Ramble has beaten the bush. Loveday is interested only in Mrs. Dashwell; Ramble is an insatiable wencher with catholic tastes; and Townly is an epicure who prefers the delights of wine to the pleasures of venery, but is always ready to taste a well-made dish. Given all these stock characters, any experienced playgoer could have foretold the outcome of the farce.

The plot, a tumbling succession of episodes, almost defies narration, but a few major sequences are worth examination. For example, Ramble, who is just ready to go to bed with "godly" Mrs. Dashwell in her own house, is frustrated by Dashwell's return. By jiggery-pokery and pretended magic, Loveday, who is in the house incognito, helps him to escape. Later, when Ramble tries to get back into the Dashwell house, he finds that his friend Townly, who happened along at the lucky minute, has anticipated him. (In the dark, and without a program, how could Mrs. Dashwell tell one rake from another?)

Later the same night, Ramble goes to keep an assignation with his second prospect, Mrs. Alderman Doodle. He is about to dance the shaking of the sheets with her when Doodle comes home and goes to bed. Ramble hides in the maid's bed in an inner room. Now the plan is for Mrs. Doodle to rise from her husband's side when Doodle is fast asleep, and come to Ramble's bed, while the maid takes her place beside the alderman. At the critical moment Ramble's stupid servant, Roger, on guard in the street, sets up a cry of fire. The household wakens; Ramble tumbles out of the house in a panic, and takes out his frustration on Roger's back with a cudgel.

When the Doodle household is quiet, Ramble tries to get back into the house, feet first through a cellar window (a forestage trap), and gets stuck. A linkboy (torchbearer) wanders by and drips hot pitch on his face. An apprentice at an upper window empties a chamberpot on his head. Two chimney sweeps blacken his face and run away with his sword, hat, and periwig. At last hauled out by the watch, Ramble is taken for a thief, jeered at by merry Mrs. Doodle, and laughed at by Townly, who ambles by, half-drunk. Yet, although humiliated and degraded, by the next night Ramble is ready for fresh adventures.

That night it is amorous Loveday's turn with godly Mrs. Dashwell. When he reveals his identity to her, she agrees to reward his constancy, but is frustrated by the sudden return of her husband. To get rid of him she tells Dashwell that Loveday has solicited her sinfully, and that she has made an assignation with him in the garden. Dressing Dashwell in woman's clothes, she sends him out to wait for Loveday and cudgel him. He goes, and she trips happily off to bed with Loveday. The sequence ends an hour or so later with Loveday, in the garden, pretending to mistake Dashwell for his wanton wife and drubbing him without mercy.

Meanwhile Alderman Doodle, who has to go away on business, commands his witty wife to say no to any impertinent fellow who dares to ask her a question. Townly meets her in Drapers Garden, quickly learns to ask the right questions, goes home with "Madam No," and has, he says, "three or four hours of the sweetest enjoyment man ever had with woman." Townly has all the luck.

Wiseacre, now married to country Peggy, also has to go out on business. He puts a gilt helmet on Peggy's head and a lance in her hand, sets his nightcap on a bed pillow, and commands her to guard it. This, he tells her, "is the duty of a wife here in London." Hardly has he left before Ramble sneaks in, persuades Peggy that Wiseacre has sent him to teach her "the whole duty of a wife," and goes to bed with her. When her husband returns, Peggy tells him all about her charming teacher and her newly acquired learning.

At the end of the farce, each of the three husbands realizes, but refuses to admit, that he is a cuckold, and each, pretending superiority, laughs at the others. Two remain doggedly faithful to their original beliefs: Dashwell would not trade his wife's "virtue" for the "wit" of Doodle's wife, and vice versa. Wiseacre tries to save face with his colleagues, but in an aside he admits that thenceforth he must keep his young wife under lock and key, "and ne'er more trust a wife's simplicity." The three citizens have their answer: whether a man has a wise wife, a pious wife, or an ignorant wife, his destiny — the forkèd plague — is still unshunnable. This is the "moral" of the play.

There is nothing startlingly new in *The London Cuckolds;* it is loaded with devices common to all cuckolding or bedroom farces. But the characters are amusing, and the dialogue, though it lacks wit and polish, is easy and often funny. If the function of farce is to make an audience laugh, this comedy, with the three citizens played by the best low comedians of the day — slab-sided Cave Underhill, shambling James Nokes, and rubicund Tony Leigh — must be counted a howling success. Perhaps it is mirth fit for clowns, but the most sophisticated audience has its clownish streak; even King Charles II enjoyed it and saw it several times. The farce was very popular in its own day, and it continued as a stage favorite for nearly a hundred years. From the end of the seventeenth century until 1751 it was customary to present *The London Cuckolds* annually at both Drury Lane and Covent Garden on Lord Mayor's Day, October 29. Such popularity had to be deserved.

Of the numerous Restoration farces, only a few merit listing with *The London Cuckolds:* Ravenscroft's *The Citizen Turned Gentleman* (1672), Newcastle's *The Triumphant Widow* (1674), D'Urfey's *Trick for Trick* (1678), Behn's *The False Count* (1681), Tate's *A Duke and No Duke* (1684), Jevon's three-act *The Devil of a Wife* (1686), and Powell's *A Very Good Wife* (1693). These are all lively, bustling, and full of fun.

Burlesque, sometimes called travesty, is farce with a critical purpose: to ridicule popular poems, novels, and plays by means of caricature, parody, and incongruity. Burlesque reduces its victim to absurdity. Because its subject is usually topical, it is inevitably ephemeral. The most famous example of Restoration burlesque is Buckingham's *The Rehearsal* (1671), "A posie made of weeds instead of flowers." Unfortunately, because the modern reader is unacquainted with the heroic plots it parodies, he misses most of the fun. Even the parodies of chosen passages, ridiculous enough in the context of the burlesque, are more effective when one has in mind the passage parodied. Here, for example, is a loving speech (an epic simile) by Almahide to her husband, Boabdelin, in *The Conquest of Granada*:

> So two kind turtles, when a storm is nigh,
> Look up, and see it gath'ring in the sky.
> Each calls his mate to shelter in the groves,
> Leaving, in murmurs, their unfinished loves.
> Perched on some drooping branch they sit alone,
> And coo, and harken to each other's moan.

In *The Rehearsal* the turtle-doves become porcine lovers:

> So boar and sow, when any storm is nigh,
> Snuff up, and smell it gath'ring in the sky;
> Boar beckons sow to trot in chestnut groves,
> And there consummate their unfinished loves.
> Pensive, in mud, they wallow all alone,
> And snort and gruntle to each other's moan.

In 1673 Thomas Duffett, a mediocre playwright employed by the King's Company, turned to caricature and produced three lively burlesques in a row. His first, *The Empress of Morocco*, "A Farce," ridiculed Settle's heroic play of the same name at the rival theater. Duffett reduced Settle's noble, heroic Moroccans to corn-cutters, draymen, porters, chimney sweeps, strong-watermen, apple-women, and cinder wenches. A long "epilogue" to the farcical *Empress* — a skit with flying witches and bawdy topical songs — made fun of the operatic version of *Macbeth*, a stock Duke's Company play. Duffett's second, *The Mock-Tempest, or The Enchanted Castle* (November, 1674), ridiculed the Davenant-Dryden-Shadwell version of Shakespeare's comedy, produced by the Duke's Company in April, 1674, as *The Tempest, or The Enchanted Island*. His third, *Psyche Debauched*

(1675), burlesqued Shadwell's elaborate opera, *Psyche,* produced by the Duke's Company some six months earlier.

According to Langbaine, in *An Account of the English Dramatic Poets* (1691), *The Mock-Tempest,* the most amusing of the three burlesques, was "writ on purpose to draw company from the other theater, where was great resort about that time to see that revived comedy called *The Tempest,* then much in vogue." Davenant and Dryden had added to Shakespeare's dramatis personae a second girl, Dorinda, who like her sister Miranda has never seen a youth; a boy, Hippolito, heir to the Duchy of Milan, who has never seen a girl; and a sister for Caliban, Sycorax. Shadwell added songs, dances, and a terminal masque of Neptune and Amphitrite. The result was pleasant musical comedy with some colorful scenes and lively tunes — delightful even to a modern audience. It has been successfully revived in recent years.

Duffett reset the opera in Bridewell, the famous London house of correction for pickpockets, harlots, and vagrants. Prospero (played by the low comedian Jo Haynes) became Prospero Whiffe, formerly Duke of the Lord Mayor's Dog Kennels and now the head keeper of Bridewell. He has a fairy assistant, Ariel (played by a gigantic orange-girl, Betty Mackerel, famed for her wit and wantonness). His two daughters, Miranda and Dorinda, are silly, sex-hungry wenches. A raid on a brothel kept by Stephania, a bawd, results in the capture and imprisonment in Bridewell of Stephania and her noise of strumpets — Beantosser, Mousetrappa, and Drinkallup — and of three customers — Alonzo, Duke of Newgate, Gonzales, and Quakero (Ferdinand), a canting nonconformist. These, of course, are Prospero Whiffe's enemies.

The burlesque is coarse, earthy, but often hilarious. It is a medley of vulgar dialogues, slapstick, stage tricks, songs, and dances, with a final ridiculous mock-masque featuring Caliban and his sister Sycorax. The parody is often very close to the original. Thus, when Prospero Whiffe imposes another task on his fairy helper, gigantic Ariel cries, "More toil! I prithee now let me remind thee of thy promise then. Where is my two-penny custard?"

PROSPERO. Ho, now, moody! dost thou murmur?
ARIEL. No, my lord.
PROSPERO. Thou liest, malignant thing, thou dost.
ARIEL. I prithee, my lord, ben't so touchy.
PROSPERO. Hast thou forgot the hairy woman I freed thee from, who sent thee every morning down her gormandizing throat with a candle and lanthorn, to tread the ooze of the salt deep? At other times she made thee pass up against the strong northern blasts, when the capacious bay was baked with brandy, till thou hadst cleared thy passage to her nose, on whose sulfurous top thou satst singing like a little chimney sweeper — hast thou forgot her?
ARIEL. No, my dread lord.
PROSPERO. If thou more murmur'st, in some small dimple of her cheek I'll peg thee, where twelve summers more thou shalt lie stewing like a maggot in a Holland cheese.
ARIEL. O pardon, great sir, this once, and I will be a good boy and never do so more.

A song which parodies Ariel's famous "Where the bee sucks, there suck I" is worth quoting as another example of Duffett's skill at reducing romance to absurdity. It was sung, of course, by big Betty Mackerel:

Where good ale is, there suck I;
In a cobbler's stall I lie,
While the watch are passing by.
Then about the streets I fly
After cullies merrily.
And I merrily, merrily take up my clothes,
Under the watch, and the constable's nose.

The brief vogue of burlesque in the 'seventies came to a close with Shadwell's parody of a typical sex intrigue comedy in the fourth act of *A True Widow* (1678), but the genre never died.

In 1697, for example, "Mr. W. M.," in *The Female Wits, or The Triumvirate of Poets at Rehearsal,* burlesqued Mrs. Manley's *The Royal Mischief* (1696), and the eighteenth century enjoyed such famous burlesques as Gay's *The Beggar's Opera* (1728), Fielding's *Tom Thumb* (1730), and Sheridan's *The Critic* (1779).

Intrigue comedy stands midway between farce and romantic tragicomedy. Every Restoration comedy has some kind of design or conspiracy as its basic story line, but intrigue comedy is dominated by a love plot; the interest lies in the poet's ingenious manipulation of amorous characters and erotic situations. As intrigue comedy ranges from farce to melodrama, it loses its laughter until, at the far end of the spectrum, it is indistinguishable from romantic melodrama or erotic tragedy with a happy ending.

In the vein of melodrama, Spanish intrigue comedies, often no more than translations from the plays of Calderón, Lope de Vega, Guillen de Castro, Moreta, and their fellows, were remarkably popular, perhaps because King Charles liked them and even suggested to playwrights that they translate or adapt certain plays for the Restoration stage. He is said to have urged Sir Samuel Tuke to adapt his successful *The Adventures of Five Hours* (1662) from a Spanish source, *Los Empeños de Seis Horas* (attributed to Calderón), and John Crowne to turn Moreto's *No Puede Ser* into the popular *Sir Courtly Nice* (1685). According to John Downes, in *Roscius Anglicanus* (1708), *The Adventures* "took successively thirteen days together, no other play intervening" — a surprisingly long run. Mr. Pepys described Tuke's comedy as "the best, for the variety and most excellent continuance of the plot to the very end, that ever I saw." Four years later he read *Othello,* "which," he said, "I ever heretofore esteemed a mighty good play, but having so lately read *The Adventures of Five Hours,* it seems a mean thing." A modern reader who takes the trouble to wade through

Tuke's long, involved, love-and-honor comedy can only conclude that Pepys was mad as a hatter.

Most Spanish intrigue comedies — translations or imitations — are romantic plays set in a Spanish city and involving a confusion of mismatched lovers, disguises, jealousies, mistaken assignations, dropped letters, overheard conversations, night scenes, serenades, and duels. The rigid code of Spanish honor is usually emphasized. In such Spanish intrigue comedies as Duffett's *The Spanish Rogue* (1673), Leanerd's *The Counterfeits* (1678), and Mountfort's *The Successful Strangers* (1689) the bustle, confusion, and complication defy analysis. Because characterization — except for an occasional "humors" character — is minimal, a modern reader, who has only the speech-tags to guide him, is likely to get lost in the complications of the plot and to dismiss such plays as tedious and dreary. The Restoration auditor, watching actors distinctively costumed, could follow the action with some ease.

English intrigue comedy, which followed the models set by Beaumont and Fletcher's gay, sophisticated plays, notably *The Scornful Lady, Rule a Wife and Have a Wife, The Chances,* and *Wit without Money,* is livelier, more realistic, and much closer to farce than the Spanish type. Usually the settings of English intrigue comedy are contemporary London scenes, but they can just as easily be French, Italian, or even Spanish. For example, Dryden's *An Evening's Love* (1668) is set in Madrid, but its characters, tone, and plot are English. Aphra Behn, who specialized in intrigue comedy, tried both English (*The Amorous Prince,* 1671, set in Florence) and Spanish types (*The Dutch Lover,* 1673, set in Madrid), and sometimes blended both with a copious sprinkling of farce, as in *The Rover* (1677).

Essential to English intrigue comedy, the staple comic fare of the Restoration playgoer, are various erotic plots, in the course of which young gallants seeking to marry or bed their sweethearts are opposed by rivals, heavy fathers, brothers, or the girls themselves. Often a cuckolding plot is woven in with marriage plots, as in Behn's *Sir Patient Fancy* (1678). The intrigues are complicated by misunderstandings, mistaken identities, and disguises — especially by girls disguised as men. For example, Southerne's *Sir Anthony Love* (1690) presents a girl disguised as a young rakehell throughout the play, and Granville's *The She-Gallants* (1695) offers two girls "in man's apparel" until the fifth act. The romantic device of a lovelorn girl dressed as a page and pursuing or serving her lover (or his mistress) was used for comic purposes in dozens of intrigue comedies; good examples are Philipa in D'Urfey's *The Royalist* (1682) and Philadelphia in Shadwell's *Bury Fair* (1689). Sometimes the plots depend upon the ingenuity of a scheming servant, like Warner in Dryden's *Sir Martin Mar-all* (1667) or Rose in Payne's *The Morning Ramble* (1672). There is usually a deal of brisk badinage and repartee, a complement of fools for farce, and often one or more mistaken marriages, or false marriages performed by mock parsons. Laughter is aroused by the unexpected twists and turns of intrigue, and by the embarrassment of the intriguers or their victims. The excellence of the comic poet is measured, not by his ability to make an incredible plot seem credible, but by his skill in selecting and fitting his episodes together, so that in the context of the play each seems credible.

George Farquhar was perhaps the last poet to write intrigue comedies according to Restoration formulas. When he came to England in 1697, fresh from the Smock Alley Theater in Dublin, his mind was well stocked with the plots of English comedies. In London he was mildly successful as an actor until by accident he wounded a fellow player in a stage duel. Thereafter he turned to writing plays. Naturally enough, in his first play, *Love and a Bottle* (1698), he used many devices which he had found in the plays he had read or had seen upon the stage.

Farquhar's rakehell, George Roebuck, is a poor but dishonest young Irishman who is "wild as winds and unconfined as air," and who wants out of life only love (i.e., sex) and a bottle. He fits the formula proposed by Lyric, Farquhar's would-be dramatic poet: "The hero in comedy is always the poet's character

. . . a compound of practical rake and speculative gentleman, who always bears off the great fortune in the play, and shams the beau and squire with a whore or chambermaid."

In Ireland Roebuck has been in love with Leanthe, sister to his friend Ned Lovewell, a wealthy young English gentleman. Because he got a whore, Trudge, with child, Roebuck has fled to London to escape Trudge's importunities and the commands of his father, who is morally so out of fashion as to insist that he marry his doxy. Roebuck encounters Lovewell in the street and begs his assistance. While the two are talking, Trudge appears with her little son. Roebuck escapes, and generous Lovewell looks after Trudge's welfare; he gives her money and sends her to lodge with the Widow Bullfinch.

While Lovewell is dickering with Trudge, his sweetheart Lucinda (eighteen, beautiful, witty, and worth twelve hundred pounds a year) sees him at his charitable exercise, leaps to the conclusion that he is paying off his own "miss," and quarrels with him. Lucinda has another suitor in reserve, Squire Mockmode, a foolish country bumpkin who has just arrived in town, lodges with Widow Bullfinch, has never seen Lucinda, and is busy learning to dance and fence.

Now the formula for intrigue comedy (according to Lyric) demands that "as the catastrophe of all tragedies is death, so the end of all comedies is marriage." ("And some think that the most tragical conclusion of the two," says Lovewell.) Therefore Lovewell must humble Lucinda's pride and marry her; Trudge must get a husband or a means of support for herself and her bastard; Squire Mockmode must be discomfited and married to "a whore or chambermaid"; and Roebuck must fall into a matrimonial snare. The snare, Lovewell's sister Leanthe, is carefully prepared and disguised. Dressed in boy's clothes, Leanthe arrived in London two weeks before Roebuck, bearing a letter to her brother, who, without recognizing her, presented her to Lucinda. Now she is serving Lucinda as a page (luscious in hose and short breeches) and fending off Lucinda's lickerish maid, Pindress.

As intriguer-in-chief, Lovewell sends Roebuck, under the name of Mockmode, to court Lucinda, and tricks the real Mockmode into courting Trudge, who poses as Lucinda. Leanthe does some ingenious plotting on her own to get Roebuck for a husband. The various plots involve mistaken identities, forged letters, a confused scene at night, and the low comedy of Lyrick with his bookseller, and foolish Mockmode with his dancing and fencing masters.

In the last act, Roebuck, in the darkness of night, marries and beds Leanthe, believing her to be Lucinda; Mockmode marries Trudge, believing her to be Lucinda; and Lucinda marries Pindress in disguise, believing her to be Roebuck in a woman's nightgown. Pindress thinks she is marrying the handsome little page. In the process of clearing up the confusion, Lovewell and Roebuck are on the verge of a duel when Leanthe comes in, dressed "in woman's loose apparel." Roebuck is delighted to learn that he has married Leanthe, his true love. Lucinda agrees to marry Lovewell if he will settle his Irish estates on Roebuck and Leanthe. Mockmode offers five hundred pounds to get out of his marriage to Trudge, whereupon the parson who performed the mock marriage is revealed as Widow Bullfinch in canonicals. Trudge gets the five hundred pounds, a fortune for an Irish whore. Everything ends happily for everyone — except poor Pindress, the maid.

As a whole, the comedy is completely preposterous. Yet the episodes are well selected and fit neatly together. Even the most incredible scene, in which Roebuck kisses "the page, love's link boy," and cries, "By heavens, this boy has the softest pair of lips I ever tasted," and still does not recognize his beloved Leanthe, is credible enough in the total comic illusion. Here the audience, because of its superior knowledge, is expected to laugh at Roebuck.

Throughout, the comedy has an air of genial good humor, as if the poet refused to take anything seriously, and looked upon his characters as delightfully interesting people who, in spite of all exaggeration, are essentially human. His laughter at the expense of his low-comedy characters — Lyrick, Mockmode, Pamphlet, Rigadoon, and Nimble-wrist — is good-natured and friendly, as if he were saying with Puck, "Lord, what fools these mortals be," and was watching their fond pageant with tolerant amusement. Farquhar loved life. Very probably Roebuck is (if not the poet's own character) what Farquhar would have liked to be — a gay, thoughtless libertine, who lives, loves, and riots to his heart's content, until he is snared at last in the net of matrimony. *Love and a Bottle* fits Farquhar's own definition of a comedy: "a well-framed tale handsomely told, as an agreeable vehicle for counsel and reproof." But he counsels only that rakehells should give up their extravagant ways of life after marrying fortunes, and he reproves only Squire Mockmode, who cannot help being a fool. He was bred at the university, where all he learned was "to guzzle fat ale, smoke tobacco, and chop logic."

Farquhar had an excellent ear for sprightly dialogue. Like all poets, he yearned to be known as a wit, and therefore he endowed his characters with sententious comments which look like the coin of wit but ring false on the counter: "He that will leave his friend for a whore, I reckon a commoner in friendship as in love." "Love, like other diseases, must sometimes have a desperate cure." "She's virtuous — and I think beauty and virtue are as ill joined as lewdness and ugliness." "Money is the sinews of love as of war." "No widow dare be seen with a poet, for fear she should be thought to keep him." Spoken briskly, these could deceive even the quickest ears in a theater.

In his nine years as a playwright ("Captain" Farquhar was born ca. 1677 and died in 1707) Farquhar wrote altogether eight comedies — originals or alterations of older plays. Of these, the best are *The Constant Couple* (1699), which quickly made him a great deal of money, just as quickly spent; *The Recruiting Officer* (1706), drawn from his own experiences on an army recruiting mission in Shropshire; and *The Beaux' Stratagem* (1707), which reflects the poet's unhappiness over his own unfortunate marriage. Often revived in modern times, *The*

Beaux' Stratagem is invariably successful because it is a play made up of sure-fire comic devices and characters, and because it has a mildly sentimental ending. As the last writer of Restoration intrigue comedy and one of the first of the new, eighteenth-century sentimental dramatists, Farquhar was a transition poet with a foot in both worlds. His comedies are neither satiric nor witty, but they are well plotted, genuinely amusing, genial, and humorous.

*** 13 ***

Humor and Satire

WHEN THOMAS SHADWELL was readying his first play, *The Sullen Lovers* (1668) for publication, he imitated his master, Ben Jonson, by adding brief character notes to the names in his dramatis personae. Thus for his two leading characters we have "Stanford, a morose, melancholy man, tormented beyond measure with the impertinence of people, and resolved to leave the world to be quit of them," and for Stanford's opposite number, "Emilia, of the same humor with Stanford."

In the modern world, "humor" is a term which includes any character, situation, story, speech, or jest which moves us to laughter. In the seventeenth century "humor" had a more limited meaning. The word came originally from medieval physiology, which asserted that a man's temperament was determined by the four fluids (humors) in his body: blood (sanguis), choler (yellow bile), melancholy (black bile) and phlegm. In a healthy man the fluids were well balanced. If one humor predominated over the others, a man could become unbalanced; he could be sanguine, choleric, melancholy, or phlegmatic. Moreover, because of the close relationship between the humors and the passions, traits allied to the humors could rule, and a man could be, for example, predominantly vain, jealous, lustful, covetous, miserly, boastful, envious, fatuous, or, like Shadwell's Sir Positive At-all, impertinently conceited. In comedy men so dominated were called "humors" characters.

In his induction to *Every Man Out of His Humor* (1599), Ben Jonson explained the humors theory of comedy. After listing the body fluids, he said of humor,

> Now thus far
> It may by metaphor apply itself
> Unto the general disposition;
> As when some one peculiar quality
> Doth so possess a man that it doth draw
> All his affects, his spirits, and his powers,
> In their conflictions, all to run one way,
> This may be truly said to be a humor.

Jonson conceived his comic characters in terms of a ruling trait or passion, and he conceived of comedy as resulting from the contrasts and conflicts between a number of such humors characters. In his own day he had many imitators, but the true humors characters rapidly disappeared and were followed by characters distinguished merely by oddities of speech, dress, or manner. The humor-names for characters which Jonson used as keys to ruling traits — Downright, Brainworm, Morose, Subtle, Sir Amorous La-Foole, Sir Epicure Mammon, and Dol Common — degenerated into mere tags descriptive of appearances and occupations. Tag names, or label names (the terms are synonymous), had at least the merit of aiding an audience, which had no printed programs, to recognize and identify stage characters.

In his preface to *The Sullen Lovers,* Shadwell, a university graduate and a man of some learning who liked to call himself one of the later "sons of Ben," pleaded for a return to the Jonsonian humors concept in comedy, and in his epilogue to *The Humorists* (1671) he re-defined the term:

> A humor is a bias of the mind,
> By which, with violence, 'tis one way inclined;
> It makes our actions lean on one side still,
> And, in all changes, that way bends the will.

Dryden, too, was interested in the humors concept. In *Of Dramatic Poesy* (1668) he defined the term in magisterial fashion. "By humor is meant some extravagant habit, passion, or affection, particular . . . to some one person, by the oddness of which he is immediately distinguished from the rest of men; which being lively and naturally represented, most frequently begets that malicious pleasure in the audience which is testified by laughter." But Dryden was careful to point out the difference between a humor and a fully developed, individualized comic character, which is a blend of many qualities. Thus Falstaff is not a humors character, "but a miscellany of humors or images, drawn from so many several men."

Few Restoration writers followed Shadwell in his slavish devotion to humors, most of them preferring to work, on the one hand, for farce, and on the other for intrigue and wit. They used the term "humors" freely, and boasted in their prefaces and prologues about the new humors they had found and presented, but usually they confused humors with mannerisms, foibles, and fashions. In his own later comedies, even Shadwell departed from his cherished precepts; inevitably he ran out of new humors and had to fall back on oddities or eccentricities. In the prologue to *Bury Fair* (1689) Shadwell complained,

> To what hard laws you comic writers bind!
> Who must at every turn new humor find;
> Though the great masters of the former age
> Had all the choice of humor for the stage,
> And they that plenteous harvest reaped so clean
> Their successors can little else but glean.

All this fuss and pother was over what is loosely called today the humor of character, a variety of incongruity which, one step higher than that resulting from physical incongruity, is the heart of all true comedy. Any eccentric or unusual character who deviates enough from the usually accepted norm to be noticed can be presented as ridiculous. If his deviation is so extreme as to require a strait-jacket, he is pathetic; but between the normality of human behavior which men have agreed to call sanity and the abnormality which requires physical restraint there is room for many kinds and degrees of incongruous, and therefore comic, characters. Thus timid men are ridiculous to the brave (that is, all the rest of us); ignorant men to the learned; boastful men to the modest; henpecked men to the masterful; effeminate men to the masculine; miserly men to the generous; and fools to the wise. The comedy of ignorance, for example, is one of the simplest and most obvious varieties of humor. Illiterate, naive, countrified, slow-witted, or scatterbrained characters provoke by their mistakes the knowing laughter of superiority. In the hands of genius, the result can be someone like Sheridan's Mrs. Malaprop.

The Restoration humors character, dominated by a single trait, was so sharply incongruous that he became, in effect, a caricature, useful for satiric and reformatory purposes. In *The Sullen Lovers* Shadwell attacked some of the more spectacular follies of his world as embodied in humor characters. In addition to melancholy, splenetic Stanford and Emilia, he included in his dramatis personae sanguine Lovel, "an airy young gentleman," and Carolina (Emilia's younger sister), "of the same humor with Lovel" — the only characters who seem to have the poet's approval and who set a *beau monde* norm for the play. Then we have Ninny, "a conceited poet" who quotes his own bad verse and "uses such affected words that 'tis as bad as the canting of a gypsy"; Woodcock, "a familiar loving coxcomb" who sings idiotic songs; Huffe, "an impudent, cowardly hector"; Lady Vaine, "a whore that takes upon her the name of a lady"; and Sir Positive At-all, "a foolish knight that pretends to understand everything in the world" and claims to be the greatest musician, politician, painter, magician, pimp, playwright, lawyer, general, linguist, shipwright, and mathematician in the world. He is indeed "a *unis in omnibus* through all the arts and sciences."

The plot is trivial. Because Carolina cannot marry until her older sister is disposed of, she connives with Lovel to throw Emilia and Stanford together at every opportunity and to vex them with the impertinences of fools, hoping to torment them into marriage. After long and cautious sparring, Emilia and Stanford discover that their humors are akin and join in melancholy matrimony. Careless Lovel and madcap Carolina banter their way into wedlock. Woodcock and Ninny, suitors for Emilia's hand, are discomfited when she discloses her marriage to Stanford. Sir Positive finds that his knowledge is not all-embracing; he marries Lady Vaine, only to learn that she has been the mistress of an anonymous keeper, by whom she has had one child and is "half gone of another." "Well," says Sir Positive aside, "this is the first thing in the world that I have met with, which I did not understand." But, true to his humor, he brazens it out, declaring that he knew what he was doing when he married. "He's a wise man that marries a harlot, he's on the surest side. Who but an ass would marry an uncertainty?"

No doubt the malicious pleasure of the audience was increased by the knowledge that Sir Positive was a caricature of a well-known politician, poet, and man-about-town, Sir Robert Howard. When Mr. Pepys saw the play at the Duke's House on May 2, 1668, he was not impressed. It had, he said, "many good humors in it, but the play tedious, and no design at all in it." He saw it again on May 4 and thought it "a very contemptible play, though there are many little witty expressions in it; and the pit did generally say that of it." When he saw it again the next day, everyone had heard the rumor that Sir Positive represented Sir Robert Howard — "And to see the folly how the house do this day cry up the play more than yesterday! and I for that reason like it, I find, the better too." Later his admiration for the play increased when he heard the Duke of York and his gentlemen maintain that the portrait of Sir Robert as Sir

Positive was "most exactly true." Mr. Pepys was ever the sedulous ape to his betters; six weeks afterward, when he saw a revival of the comedy, he commented, "A pretty good play." His first judgment was sounder.

Fat Thomas Shadwell, whose chief diversion was to sit drinking ale with his friends, was neither a genius nor the dull sot of Dryden's *Mac Flecknoe.* He was a doctrinaire writer, cramped by the rigidity of his formula. In his preface to *The Sullen Lovers* — which is long on "humors" and short on humor — he admitted that the comedy lacked plot and that "there is the same thing over and over," but he justified both faults on the ground of his intention: "to represent variety of humors" in order to satirize vice and folly. The modern reader looks in vain for some kind of an intrigue or for fully developed characters, and soon tires of the noisy fops, braggarts, and fools, who return to the scene again and again to show off their humors.

In the course of his career as a poet Shadwell learned eventually that humors characters alone could not satisfy a Restoration audience. As Dryden pointed out in the preface to *An Evening's Love,* "to entertain an audience perpetually with humor is to carry them from the conversation of gentlemen, and treat them with the follies and extravagance of Bedlam." In his best comedies — such plays as *Bury Fair* (1689) and *The Volunteers* (1692) — Shadwell employed most of the plot devices of intrigue comedy, headed his dramatis personae with gentlemen "of wit and pleasure" and ladies of "wit, beauty, and fortune" (one looks in vain for the wit), and relegated his humors to lower-class or minor characters. In *Bury Fair,* for example, he has two pairs of attractive lovers, Lord Bellamy and Philadelphia (serving Lord Bellamy as a page), and Wildish and Gertrude. His humors characters are Mr. Oldwit, an old-fashioned "wit"; Sir Humphrey Noddy, a crude practical joker; Mr. Trim, a ceremonious fop; and Lady Fantast and her daughter, who are disgustingly vain of their wit and breeding. Appropriately, they are gulled by a French peruke maker disguised as a count.

Shadwell is often described as a realist, and it is true that the humors method of characterization lends itself to a realistic bias, to the synthesis and interpretation of normal human experience. But he dealt rather with the abnormal, with rogues, knaves, and fools. In response to his successful "realistic" comedy, *The Squire of Alsatia* (1688), which exploited the sharpers and bullies of the London underworld, a courtier, Peregrine Bertie, remarked, "There is nothing in it extraordinary — except it is a Latin song — but the thin reason why it takes so well is because it brings several of the cant words upon the stage which some in town have invented, and turns them into ridicule." This is first-rate journalism, not realism.

Shadwell had a sharp eye for the surface of lower-class contemporary life, a good ear for vulgar conversation, and considerable skill at reproducing what he saw and heard. He presented a wide variety of fops, fools, bumpkins, lechers, sharpers, knaves, whores, and cowards, but his attitude toward them was narrowly moralistic; he never organized them into a rounded interpretation of human experience. His plays are often heavily amusing, but his plots are loose and his characters are, in the main, only two-dimensional; in his gallery of humors there are no memorable portraits. Perhaps his heaviness was consonant with his physical bulk. Irreverent Tom Brown is the supposed author of this triplet, written when Shadwell (who had replaced Dryden as poet laureate) died in 1692:

> And must our glorious laureate then depart?
> Heaven, if it please, may take his loyal heart,
> As for the rest, sweet Devil, bring a cart.

In *An Allusion to Horace* (1676), John Wilmot, Earl of Rochester, the literary leader of the Court Wits and a notable Jonsonian himself, found only two contemporary comic writers worthy of praise:

> Of all our modern wits, none seems to me
> Once to have touched upon true comedy

> But hasty Shadwell and slow Wycherley.
> Shadwell's unfinished works do yet impart
> Great proofs of force of Nature, none of art;
> With just bold strokes he dashes here and there,
> Showing great mastery with little care;
> And scorns to varnish his good touches o'er
> To make the fools and women praise 'em more.
> But Wycherley earns hard whate'er he gains;
> He wants no judgment, nor he spares no pains;
> He frequently excels, and at the least,
> Makes fewer faults than any of the best.

Like Shadwell, slow William Wycherley used humors characters for satiric purposes, but he developed them more completely, and he wore his wormwood with a difference. Shadwell stood thick-legged on the stony foundation of Christian morality. Wycherley, a handsome young libertine, took his stance in the rank soil of libertine naturalism, which excluded the supernatural. Skeptical of all religions and moralities, Wycherley admired only those who, true to their natural, animal selves, sought pleasure as the sole good in life; he lashed with satire all pretenders and hypocrites. Like most of the Court Wits he was a rational hedonist. In terms of sex, his ideal society anticipated that of Huxley's *Brave New World,* in which "everyone belongs to everyone else," and love is only a fig leaf to cover naked lust. "Ceremony in love," said Wycherley's Horner, "is as ridiculous as in fighting; falling on briskly is all should be done on such occasions."

A better playwright than Shadwell, Wycherley wrote only four comedies: *Love in a Wood* (1671), which brought him favor at Court and the love of the Duchess of Cleveland, the King's cast mistress; *The Gentleman Dancing Master* (1672); *The Country Wife* (1675); and *The Plain Dealer* (1676), which, after its protagonist, gave him the nickname he bore to the end of his days, "Manly" Wycherley.

In *The Country Wife,* Wycherley's most entertaining comedy, only Horner, the natural man, and his witty friends, Harcourt and Dorilant, escape the shafts of satire. As his name suggests, Horner ("A comely person") is a cuckold maker, who delights in equipping husbands with the horns symbolic of their betrayal. He pursues and captures women for his pleasure, even while despising them for their silliness and precise hypocrisy. But he is not an ordinary lecher; he is "a Machiavel in love," who enjoys a well-laid plot as much as a woman. He is a generous man, a good friend, and a wit who thinks that "wit is more necessary than beauty," and that no young woman is "ugly that has it, and no handsome woman [is] agreeable without it."

To gain access to the hen-roosts of the Town, Horner, aided by Dr. Quack, an unscrupulous physician, persuades his friends and acquaintances (especially the husbands and guardians of desirable young women) that he has become impotent as the result of venereal disease and the malpractice of a French surgeon. By this device, he gets the privileges of a eunuch with the ironically named "virtuous gang"—Lady Fidget (wife of Sir Jasper Fidget, a City knight) and her two unmarried friends, Mrs. Dainty Fidget and Mrs. Squeamish. Each of the three is admitted privately into Horner's secret, that he is decidedly not "an arrant French capon"; each accepts him as a lover with clucks of joy and for most of the play believes herself to be his only mistress.

A lesser dramatist would have shown us each of Horner's conquests in luscious detail. Wycherley appeals to our imaginations. We can easily guess what will follow when Horner privately tells Lady Fidget the truth about his undiminished sexual powers, and she whispers, "But, poor gentleman, could you be so generous, so truly a man of honor, as for the sakes of us women of honor to cause yourself to be reported no man? No man! and to suffer yourself the greatest shame that could fall upon a man, that none might fall upon us women by your conversation? But [are you] indeed, sir, as perfectly, perfectly the same man as before your going into France, sir? As perfectly, perfectly, sir? . . . Nay, then, as one may say, you may do your worst, dear, dear sir!"

Wycherley got his best effects by obvious *double entendre*. In the famous "china scene," for instance (IV,3), Lady Fidget and Horner are interrupted in Horner's lodgings by the arrival of Sir Jasper Fidget. Not to be balked of her desires, Lady Fidget goes into Horner's bedchamber, pretending to be in search of a piece of china. Horner follows through another exit, and Sir Jasper calls through the chamber door, "Wife! My Lady Fidget! Wife! he is coming in to you the back way!"

LADY FIDGET (*off-stage*). Let him come and welcome, which way he will.

SIR JASPER. He'll catch you and use you roughly, and be too strong for you.

LADY FIDGET. Don't you trouble yourself, let him if he can.

Dr. Quack, hiding behind a screen on the stage, can hardly believe his eyes and ears.

Sir Jasper, the complacent cuckold, guards Horner's chamber door against two later guests, Mrs. Squeamish and her grandmother, Old Lady Squeamish. When Lady Fidget re-enters with a piece of china in her hand and Horner following, Mrs. Squeamish insists that she must have some china too, but Horner replies honestly, "Upon my honor, I have none left now."

We are not at all surprised when we learn that all three of "the virtuous gang," who constantly proclaim their honor and their hatred of smut, filth, and whores, have had Horner's porcelain — and his contempt. In a bibulous moment, when the three biddies discover that each has shared Horner's perch, they are confounded. "Well, then," says Lady Fidget, "there's no remedy, sister sharers; let us not fall out but have a care of our honor, the jewel of most value and use, which shines yet to the world unsuspected, though it be counterfeit." Since honor, like beauty, depends only on the opinion of others, the three "false rogues" feel safe enough.

However, a fourth bird has her eye on Horner. Margery Pinchwife is a plump, young country chick married to old

Pinchwife, a retired rakehell whose name describes his jealous humor, and who has not heard of Horner's "English-French disaster." Margery falls in love with Horner, tricks her husband into delivering a letter to him, and later tricks him into conveying her to Horner's lodgings disguised as Pinchwife's sister, Alithea. Country-bred Margery, whose morality is drawn from the barnyard, is a fair match for Horner. By nature and breeding she is as much a natural woman as by conviction he is a natural man.

Much to her delight, Margery finds that Horner is a mettled gamecock. She refuses to leave his lodgings after consummation, and declares that she will have Horner as her husband. In the final discovery scene the comedy skirts along the edges of disaster as Dr. Quack, Horner's friends, and the members of "the virtuous gang" try to persuade Pinchwife that he cannot be a cuckold because Horner is a eunuch. Silly Mistress Margery almost blows the game. When Dorilant calls Horner a capon, she cries, " 'Tis false, sir! You shall not disparage poor Mr. Horner, for to my certain knowledge — " Fortunately, Lucy, a maidservant, shuts her up before she can let the cat out of the bag.

A subplot involving Pinchwife's sister, Alithea, seems at first glance incongruous. Alithea, a woman of wit and fashion, who takes "the innocent liberty of the Town" untouched by scandal, stands out like white-robed purity against the lustful hypocrites of her sex. But Wycherley had a satiric purpose in creating her. Her brother has betrothed her to Sparkish, a smug, conceited fool, who "can no more think the men laugh at him than that women jilt him, his opinion of himself is so good." Horner's friend Harcourt meets Alithea, falls honorably in love with her, and in some amusing scenes does his best to break off her match with Sparkish and marry her himself. But, although Alithea is attracted by Harcourt's "person and understanding," she is foolishly true to her conception of honor. "But what a devil is this honor?" asks Lucy, her maid, " 'tis sure a disease in the head, like the megrim or falling-sickness, that always hurries people away to do themselves mischief. Men lose their lives by it; women, what's dearer to 'em, their love, the life of life." Nevertheless Alithea insists on keeping her word to Sparkish, who, with all his faults, has at least one merit in her eyes: he is never jealous. Later, when Sparkish, believing her false to him with Horner, shows himself in his true colors as a petty, jealous fool, she breaks her engagement gladly and goes in search of Harcourt. But before leaving the stage, she delivers a warning homily to the audience:

> And now I wish that if there be any overwise women of the Town, who, like me, would marry a fool for fortune, liberty, or title, first that her husband may love play and be a cully to all the Town but her and suffer none but Fortune to be mistress of his purse; then, if for liberty, that he may send her into the country under the conduct of some huswifely mother-in-law; and if for title, may the world give 'em none but that of cuckold.

Unlike most Restoration comedies, *The Country Wife* ends with only one marriage in prospect: that of Alithea and Harcourt. Presumably Horner will go his merry, cuckold-making way, and sport with scores of Lady Fidgets in the shade of his reputation as a eunuch. Pinchwife, cursed by jealousy, will always wonder what happened in Horner's lodgings, and little Margery will be a country wife again because she cannot, she learns, like a city wife, free herself from her musty husband and do as she pleases.

Wycherley's plot is clearly conceived and executed. Most of his characters are so fully developed that their "humors" bases are not readily apparent. His dialogue is brisk and vigorous, but his efforts at wit — similitudes and epigrams — are usually strained, as if he had labored painfully to give them birth. In spite of Macaulay's decree that Wycherley's "indecency . . . is too filthy to handle and too noisome even to approach," *The Country Wife* has been revived frequently in the twentieth century, with great applause and without moral objection. Morals, like manners, change with the times.

Since Wycherley drew much of his material for *The Country Wife* from Molière's *L'École des Femmes* and *L'École des Maris*, it is not surprising that for his fourth and last comedy, *The Plain Dealer* (December, 1676), he turned to another of Molière's comedies, *Le Misanthrope*. Molière believed that the greatest enemy of mankind was not folly but hypocrisy, and through his protagonist, misanthropic Alceste, he raked the hypocrites of his age with broadsides of satire. Alceste's ideal world, like that of Wycherley's Manly, was one in which absolute sincerity controlled all human relations. But there the resemblance ends. Manly is not a misanthrope, and Wycherley is not an English Molière.

The dramatis personae of *The Plain Dealer* describes Manly as "of an honest, surly, nice humor" — i.e., a frank, morose, and discriminating natural man — who, in the time of the (Second?) Dutch War chose "a sea-life only to avoid the world." Before he sailed in command of a convoy to the West Indies, Manly consigned five or six thousand pounds' worth of gold and jewels to the care of his sweetheart, Olivia, and consigned Olivia to the care of his bosom friend, Vernish, who promptly, and secretly, married her. When his ship was sunk in a battle with the Dutch, Manly lost the other half of his fortune: goods worth another five or six thousand pounds with which he had planned to settle in the West Indies, where Olivia was to join him later. As the play opens, Manly has just returned to London after a month's absence at sea. Although he is pestered by fops and fools who profess friendship, Manly's only real friends are his merry lieutenant, Freeman, "a complier with the age," and his page, Fidelia, a girl disguised as a boy, Manly's "little volunteer," who loves, follows, and serves him. But headstrong Manly refuses to accept their friendship, and believes that his only true friends are Olivia and Vernish. In the course of the play he is painfully disillusioned.

To his sailors, Manly is a hero, a "bully tar," "rough and angry," "a hurry-durry blade," who lives for honor and is pleased only by war. Freeman loves and admires him, and offers his sincere friendship. To Fidelia, Manly is the "bravest, worthiest of mankind." "Fame, the old liar," she tells him, "is believed when she speaks wonders of you. You cannot be flattered, sir; your merit is unspeakable." Even Olivia, secretly his bitterest enemy, admits that he has a "great spirit." Among his virtues, generosity is not the least. He gives his last twenty pounds — all he has in the world — to his boat's crew, because he cannot bear to see "the poor, honest, brave fellows want."

Manly's likeness to the typical protagonist of heroic drama is unmistakable. He is intensely masculine (hence "Manly"), a fierce fighter, a rugged individualist, rough and blunt, devoted to honor and intolerant of cowards, liars, sycophants, and supple courtiers. So was plain-dealing Almanzor in Dryden's *The Conquest of Granada.* Manly esteems a lord no more than Almanzor esteems a king, and neither cares a fig for titles without "intrinsic worth." Manly, like Almanzor, is passionately in love, but, unlike Almanzor, he loves a woman whom we know to be unworthy, Olivia, a mercenary jilt. In this respect he is more nearly akin to the secondary heroes in *The Conquest,* Abdalla and Abdelmelech, who love another mercenary jilt, Lyndaraxa. To complete the parallel, just as evil Lyndaraxa is contrasted with chaste, loyal Almahide (or with pretty little Benzayda, who once dons boy's clothes), so evil Olivia is contrasted with loyal, loving Fidelia. Finally, Vernish, who proves to be as evil within as he is smooth without, is comparable to the typical villain of heroic drama, for example, to Zulema, in *The Conquest.*

The fact that Manly has been deceived by Olivia is no reflection on his judgment. Hypocritical Olivia (like Lyndaraxa) is an artist at deceit; she deceives her lover, Manly; her husband, Vernish; and two suitors, Novel and Lord Plausible. Moreover, again like Lyndaraxa, she is very beautiful, and her form, says Manly, "would make a starved hermit a ravisher." Even after he discovers (in II,i) that Olivia has cheated him, that she never loved him, that she wanted only his money (which she refuses to return), and that in his absence she has married a gentleman whom she refuses to name, Manly still loves and desires her. So too, even after he is aware of wicked Lyndaraxa's hypocrisy, heroic Abdelmelech is still a slave to his love for her.

For Abdelmelech's "heroical love," the only cure was death. To cure Manly, Wycherley turned to the prescriptions of a popular physician, Robert Burton, who, in *The Anatomy of Melancholy,* advised, "The last and best cure of love-melancholy is to let them have their desires." As a victim of love-melancholy, Manly is in a bad way and, much against his will, has to turn hypocrite himself to conceal his passion from his lieutenant, Freeman. To his page he half-bares his heart. He cannot live without Olivia, he insists; and then, shamefacedly, declares that he must lie with her for revenge. He orders Fidelia to pimp for him, and threatens her with banishment if she refuses. The "little volunteer" goes out sadly and returns some time later to deliver to her master insulting messages from his former sweetheart and the bitter news that she herself has barely escaped the lecherous clutches of Olivia, "who has impudence enough to put a court out of countenance and debauch a stews." Manly cries, "Damned, damned woman, that could be so false and infamous! and damned, damned heart of mine, that cannot yet be false, though so infamous! what easy, tame, suffering, trampled things does that little god of talking cowards make us!" But he is still a slave to passion.

Olivia has forced the epicene page to promise to return "within this hour, as soon as it should be dark." Manly goes with her and, in the dusk of Olivia's lodgings, exchanges identities with Fidelia, goes to bed with Olivia, and has his surfeit of her. In the context of Restoration comedy he has done nothing dishonorable. By her vicious conduct, Olivia has put herself beyond the pale of honor. Poor Fidelia, forced to stay and "act the second part of a lover," is caught by Vernish, who discovers her sex ("Pulls off her peruke and feels her breasts") and is only by accident prevented from ravishing her.

Manly's treatment works; now his love-melancholy is cured, and he is once more a hero in command of himself and the situation. To revenge himself on Olivia and expose her to the world, he arranges to substitute for Fidelia again the next night, and tells Freeman to bring witnesses at a predetermined time. However, he makes the mistake of telling Vernish, whom he still believes to be his friend, that he has an appointment with Olivia. Nonetheless, his plot succeeds. Olivia is surprised in his arms; Vernish, his bosom friend, is disclosed as her bloody-minded husband; and Fidelia, whose periwig has fallen off in a scuffle, is discovered to be a beautiful woman. Manly gets his revenge, his gold and jewels, and the hand of Fidelia Grey, an heiress with an income of two thousand pounds a year. Still a surly, blunt hero, to whom the world is just as "odious" as ever, Manly concludes that after the testimonies he has seen,

> there are now in the world
> Good-natured friends, who are not prostitutes,
> And handsome women worthy to be friends.

For Fidelia's sake, then, he decides that he "will remain in this ill world of ours still." After all, even a bitter satire can close on a pleasant note.

The Plain Dealer, then, is a serious satiric play, which, like all true satire, verges upon tragedy. In the critical division of the dramatis personae, only Manly, Fidelia, and Freeman win some measure of the poet's approval. The play is equipped with a hero, Manly, a heroine, Fidelia, and a pair of precious villains, Olivia and Vernish, to be exposed and punished. Vernish has stolen Manly's mistress and money, and, with the unfair aid of a dark lantern to dazzle Manly, he has tried to take his friend's life. Too wicked for the shafts of satire, he is comic in only one scene, when Manly tells him how he has cuckolded Olivia's unidentified husband, and Vernish (the husband) has to conceal his chagrin. Olivia is both comic character and, incongruously, villainess. She is ridiculed as an affected misanthrope who claims to be weary of "the filthy world," as a prude so revolted by the china scene in *The Country Wife* that she has broken all her own china, and as a hypocrite who loves malicious gossip while pretending that gossip is her "aversion." In her villainess role she is shown to be vulgar, vicious, mercenary, and lustful to the point of nymphomania. As a dramatic character she is loaded with too many incompatible traits to be completely credible.

Only loosely connected with the main plot is a cluster of ridiculous humors characters: Novel, "an admirer of novelties"; Lord Plausible, "a ceremonious, supple, commending coxcomb"; and Major Oldfox (old blade), "an old, impertinent fop" who pursues Widow Blackacre, "a petulant, litigious widow," whose great love is lawsuits and litigation. Lieutenant Freeman pursues her also, and eventually blackmails her into giving him an allowance of three hundred pounds a year. Widow Blackacre seems to be a feminine version of Wycherley's father, Daniel, who also delighted in lawsuits.

In addition, Wycherley gives us a swarm of unpleasant types who represent their occupations rather than their humors. A Lawyer, an Alderman, and two Knights of the Post — hired witnesses and forgers — are fairly conventional; but the numerous gentlemen of the long robe whom Manly meets in Westminster Hall seem to reflect Wycherley's experience as a law student at the Inns of Court. Lawyers are fair game to any generation, but Ploddon, Quaint, Blunder, Petulant, Buttongown, and Splitcause are truly horrible examples of the legal profession. Wycherley, who had spent many weary months at the Inner Temple, was well acquainted with the shifts and cheats of barristers. But he exposed his victims, not for moral reasons — his mind was too ironic for morality — but for practical, worldly reasons. He seemed intent on warning his audience against the crafty practices and deceits of lawyers, litigants, courtiers, politicians, and paid witnesses.

In the world of modern criticism there has been "much violent throwing about of brains" over the nature of Manly's character and his dramatic function. Some critics have argued that Manly is identifiable with Wycherley himself, a Puritan and "a ferocious moralist." (According to all accounts, Wycherley was genial, kindly, tolerant, and good-tempered.) Others have argued that Manly is a "Truewit" *manqué,* or a deluded, self-righteous egotist, or a comic humors character and a butt for Wycherley's satire. Surely the fact that the author of *The Plain Dealer* was known as "Manly" Wycherley, a name which he accepted complacently, is enough to show that in the Restoration Manly was regarded as an admirable character. For many years after the first production of the play, playgoers and critics joined in singing Wycherley's praises. For example, Dryden, who rarely praised a rival, said in his preface to *The State of Innocence* (printed in 1677), "Satire lashes vice into reformation, and humor represents folly so as to make it ridiculous. Many of our present writers are eminent in both these kinds; and particularly the author of *The Plain Dealer,* whom I am proud to call my friend, has obliged all honest and virtuous men by one of the most bold, most general, and most useful satires which has ever been presented on the English theater."

There were, indeed, many writers eminent at depicting humors of a sort, including Dryden himself, the Duke of Newcastle, Aphra Behn, Thomas Ravenscroft, and, especially, Thomas D'Urfey, a prolific writer of farces loaded with trifling humors and social types. But most Restoration playwrights lacked the indignation requisite for satire; even Dryden's *The Kind Keeper* is more farce than fury. Some comic writers dealt in personal or particular satire. Shadwell attacked Sir Robert Howard and Robert Hooke; Arrowsmith lampooned Dryden as a comic Tutor in *The Reformation* (1673); Chamberlayne pilloried Elkanah Settle as Sir Symon Credulous and Ravenscroft as Sir Jasper Sympleton in *Wits Led by the Nose* (1677); and D'Urfey libeled Lady Mary Fenwick as Lady Addleplot in *Love for Money* (1690). Of course political satires flourished in the years 1679–1690. Of these, Crowne's *City Politiques* (1683), a satire on identifiable Whig leaders, is especially noteworthy because it inspired a very early example of the newspaper review. Under the date of January 20, 1683, a journalist wrote:

> Yesterday was acted at the Theater Royal the first of a new play entitled the City Politiques, the novelty of which drew a confluence of spectators under both qualifications of Whig and Tory to hear and behold a Lord Mayor, Sheriffs, and some Aldermen with their wives in their usual formalities buffooned and reviled; a great lawyer with his young lady jeered and intrigued; Dr. Oates perfectly represented, berogued and beslaved; the papist plot egregiously ridiculed; the Irish testimonies contradictorily disproved and befooled; the Whigs totally vanquished and undone; law and property men overruled; and there wanted nothing of artifice in behavior or discourse to render all those obnoxious and despised. In fine, such a medley of occurrences intervened that 'twas a question whether more of loyalty, design, or rhetoric prevailed, but there were mighty clappings among the people of both parties in expressing either their satisfaction or displeasure.

One looks in vain among the political and topical satires of these years for such a bold, general, useful satire as *The Plain Dealer,* with its stinging attacks on the greed, lust, and hypocrisy of the Restoration world.

*** 14 ***

The Comedy of Wit

PHYSICAL COMEDY and character (or humors) comedy depend upon incongruities. The comedy of wit depends upon the revelation of unsuspected congruities, or likenesses. Wit, said Thomas Hobbes, in *The Leviathan,* is an intellectual virtue. "Natural wit consisteth principally in two things; celerity of imagining (that is, swift succession of one thought to another) and steady direction to some approved end. . . . In this succession of man's thoughts . . . those that observe their similitudes, in case they be such as are but rarely imagined by others, are said to have a good wit, by which, in this occasion, is meant a good fancy. But they that observe their differences and dissimilarities . . . are said to have a good judgment. . . . This virtue is called discretion." A century later, Dr. Johnson, discussing the seventeenth-century metaphysical poets, defined wit as "the unexpected copulation of ideas, the discovery of some occult relation between images in appearance remote from each other," or, more philosophically, "a kind of *discordia concors,* a combination of dissimilar images."

Necessary for comic wit, then, as separate from "wit written . . . a propriety of thoughts and words," is fancy controlled by judgment or discretion. Comic wit gives pleasure by the unexpected but pertinent association of seeming incongruities. It is usually expressed in clever "turns," similitudes, word-plays (puns), allusions, epigrams, or irony. "Our love is frail as is our life and full as little in our power." " 'Tis better to be left than never to have been loved." "A gamester will be a gamester whilst his money lasts, and a whoremaster whilst his vigor." "The coldness of a losing gamester lessens the pleasure of winning." "Beauty runs as great a risk exposed at Court as wit does on the stage, where the ugly and the foolish all are free to censure." The ladies "come together like the coroner's inquest to sit upon the murdered reputations of the week." "Ah, dear Marwood, what's integrity to an opportunity?"

Comic wit is concerned with ideas; its appeal is essentially intellectual. Uncontrolled by discretion, fancy can run wild with pointless puns, quibbles, persiflage, and rambling, extravagant nonsense to please the ears of the groundlings. Fancy controlled by judgment results in true wit — subtle, penetrating, and illuminating — which can move one (in Dryden's phrase) "to a pleasure that is more noble" than that provided by humor. Witty repartee, said Dryden, is one of the chief graces of comedy: "The greatest pleasure of the audience is in a chase of wit kept up on both sides and swiftly managed." The Restoration was obsessed with wit, and its poets and critics wore out the word with endless repetition.

Definitions are pretty, but no man becomes a wit by following a formula. A true wit is born, not made. He may sharpen his native fancy by practice, by reading, writing and conversing, and he may, with maturity, learn discretion, but a quick and lively fancy is a gift from the gods. Perhaps the taste for wit is a gift also. Certainly it cannot be acquired by the serious-minded, to whom Restoration wit comedy is likely to seem "trivial, gross, and dull."

The comedy of wit was written for a drawing-room society — the *beau monde* — not for those who expected comedy to provide a serious criticism of life. It is often called comedy of manners because it deals with mannered people, those to the manner born. It was written for people who prided themselves on their intellectuality, their sophistication, and their *savoir vivre.* They lived in a constricted world, from which weighty problems were rigidly barred, perhaps because no one knew the answers. They were interested in the subtleties of human relationships within their enclave, and they prized the interpretations of those relationships through the blend of fancy and judgment which they called wit. Descriptive criticism fails in its function when it refuses to see their art in terms of their intellectual demands and standards.

The best wits were those who belonged to the coterie. Consider Sir George Etherege, born plain George, called "Gentle" George by his friends, and dubbed knight by King Charles II after he married a rich widow (ca. 1680). He seems to have spent his youth in Paris, where he acquired the language, graces, and manners of a true Parisian. Returning to England about 1663, he became a man-about-town. He wrote a play, *The Comical Revenge, or Love in a Tub* (1664). Its success brought him a berth in the Duke of York's band of gentleman pensioners and membership in the inner circle of Court Wits — Buckingham, Rochester, Dorset, Mulgrave, Sir Charles Sedley, Henry Savile, Henry Killigrew, Bab May, Fleetwood Shephard, William Wycherley, *et al.* He wrote another play in 1668, *She Would If She Could,* became a gentleman of the King's Privy Chamber, and went to Turkey for three years in the train of the English Ambassador to that country. He was a cultured gentleman, a courtier, and a diplomat; a skeptic by conviction, a hedonist by disposition, a deist by choice, a libertine by practice, a wit by the grace of God, and a playwright by accident. (He also wrote "airy songs and soft lampoons.") He wrote only three plays, but his third and last, *The Man of Mode, or Sir Fopling Flutter* (1676), is generally recognized as one of the best wit (or "manners") comedies of the age. According to his friend, the Earl of Rochester, Etherege was "a sheer original," and no other poet had "more fancy, sense, judgment, and wit." In *Mac Flecknoe,* Dryden praised him and his characters,

> Let Gentle George in triumph tread the stage,
> Make Dorimant betray, and Loveit rage;
> Let Cully, Cockwood, Fopling charm the pit,
> And in their folly show the writer's wit.

Some critics begged to differ. In his *News from Hell* (1681) Captain Alexander Radcliffe represented Etherege as damned,

> for writing superfine,
> With words correct in every line;
> And one that does presume to say,
> A plot's too gross for any play.
> Comedy should be clean and neat,
> As gentlemen do talk and eat.
> So what he writes is but translation
> From Dog and Partridge conversation.

The Dog and Partridge was a famous tavern in Fleet Street.

Seen superficially, the plot of *The Man of Mode* is indeed slight and obvious. Dorimant, a wencher, tries to rid himself of an old mistress, Mrs. Loveit, to acquire a new mistress, Bellinda, and to marry Harriet, an heiress from the country. He succeeds in the first two enterprises, and at the end of the play is well on his way to success in the third. The subplot deals with Young Bellair, whose father wants him to marry Harriet. Instead he secretly marries his sweetheart Emilia, with whom his foolish father, Old Bellair, fancies himself in love. Sir Fopling Flutter, the "man of mode," a plain English blockhead who has returned from France as "the pattern of modern foppery," amuses the company at Lady Townley's salon with his foibles and follies. The label names are sufficiently obvious.

But this summary ignores the subtleties and nuances of the comedy. When we read more carefully, we learn that Dorimant is the top wit of the Town — handsome, genteel, versatile, and accomplished. Lady Townley describes him as "a very well-bred man," Emilia as "a very witty man," and Bellinda as "strangely ill-natured" and "a man of no principles."

"Your man of principles is a very fine thing indeed," says Dorimant's friend Medley, ironically.

"To be preferred to men of parts," Bellinda retorts, "by women who have regard to their reputation and quiet. Well, were I minded to play the fool, he should be the last man I'd think of." Two minutes later, Dorimant comes in, takes Bellinda aside, and persuades her to visit him in his lodgings at five o'clock the next morning.

In short, Dorimant, the gilded lover, is the ideal of the Restoration coterie, one who fathoms "all the depths of woman kind," and who has a tongue that "would tempt the angels to a second fall." Dorimant is as irresistible in the boudoir as Almanzor is all-conquering on the battlefield. Yet, although he is "flesh and blood," he is not a vulgar lecher; he is a gourmet in sex who seduces women as much for the glory of the conquest as out of sexual gluttony. He delights in proving his power over women. Early in the play he complains, "I have not had the pleasure of making a woman so much as break her fan, to be sullen, or forswear herself these three days." He is inconstant, of course. When he tires of a woman, he must make it clear to his world that he has dismissed her, not vice versa. To admit that he has fallen seriously in love is to lose face; to court the banes of matrimony is to lose his standing as a wit.

Dorimant's campaign against Mrs. Loveit ("a violent creature . . . the most passionate in her love and the most extravagant in her jealousy") is itself a comic reversal of the norm. The audience was accustomed to the sight of gallants pursuing prospective mistresses; now it saw a gallant trying to get rid of his "convenient." To win Bellinda to his bed, Dorimant has promised to break off his affair with Mrs. Loveit. His reputation as a libertine wit is at stake; he must outwit his mistress and put her in the wrong. Therefore he arouses her jealousy, quarrels with her, and accuses her of a tenderness for the fool, Sir Fopling Flutter. To further his plot and to show off his power over Mrs. Loveit, he encourages Sir Fopling to woo her publicly in the Mall, where "all the world" comes at night to stroll and chat. Dorimant is certain that in his presence Mrs. Loveit will snub Sir Fopling and make "good sport." Instead, Loveit plays up to Fopling and snubs Dorimant. Medley, "the very spirit of scandal," whom Dorimant has brought along as a witness, comments mockingly, "Would you had brought some more of your friends, Dorimant, to have been witnesses of Sir Fopling's disgrace and your triumph."

Dorimant's second attempt to humiliate Loveit fails also. After spending a happy morning hour in bed with Bellinda, and promising her never to see Loveit in private again, he breaks his word and goes to Loveit's lodgings to tax her with Sir Fopling and to pluck off her mask of indifference and "show the passion that lies panting under." The battle is at its height, and Dorimant has almost persuaded Loveit to prove her love for him by snubbing Sir Fopling in public, when Bellinda enters the room. Dorimant is confounded. Faced with two angry women at once, he is at a loss for words and takes refuge in flight.

Meanwhile, although he knows that he can win Harriet only with a wedding ring, Dorimant has fallen unfashionably in love with her. Later the same day, while he is trying to persuade Harriet to marry him, Loveit and Bellinda enter Lady Townley's drawing room together. Dorimant, forced to juggle three women at once, is appalled. "The devil owes me a shame today," he says aside, "and I think never will have done paying it." But his wit rises to the occasion. As the company drifts about the stage and he gets his chance for a private conversation with one woman after another (downstage, near the footlights), he brushes off Bellinda's reproaches with a brutal jest and a hint of future meetings; placates Loveit by telling her that he seeks to marry Harriet only "to repair the ruin" of his estate (an obvious but face-saving lie); and gains permission to visit Harriet in the country as a preliminary to marriage. He wins everything, even a public demonstration of his power over

Loveit, who (still in love with Dorimant) snubs Sir Fopling viciously. Medley, who sees and knows all, sums up, "Dorimant, I pronounce thy reputation clear, and henceforward when I would know anything of woman, I will consult no other oracle."

The Man of Mode is critical, but never really satiric. Etherege was too urbane for indignation and too much an artist to descend to caricature. Thus the traditions that Dorimant was intended as a portrait of the Earl of Rochester, Medley of Sir Charles Sedley, and Sir Fopling Flutter of a well-known man about town, Sir George Hewitt, are not to be trusted. The characters are composites, representing the best and the worst in the small coterie which lived for pleasure, valued wit and good manners, distrusted passion, and laughed at fools.

The standard of values is not manners or morals but the possession of libertine wit. In the scale established by the play, Dorimant is clearly the top wit among the gentlemen; appropriately the role was created by the great actor Thomas Betterton. The other male characters can be ranked according to the degrees of their wit. Immediately below Dorimant is Medley, a pleasant man, an excellent raconteur, full of fancy, jests, and raillery. Although there is no proof of his practice, he professes libertinism. Next is Young Bellair, whom Dorimant describes as "handsome, well-bred, and by much the most tolerable of all the young men that do not abound in wit." Dorimant associates with Bellair for their mutual interests: "it makes the women think the better of his understanding, and judge more favorably of my reputation; it makes him pass upon some for a man of very good sense [wit] and I upon others for a civil person." But Young Bellair is given up for lost because he marries for love instead of money. Dorimant is wise enough to fall in love with an heiress.

Old Bellair, a stock example of the old man with delusions of glamour (created by the low comedian Tony Leigh), is very low in the scale. He is fifty-five; Emilia is perhaps fifteen or sixteen. Although he is a good-natured old fellow, he lacks the wit to realize that love — alas! — is only for youth. Sir Fopling, of course, is at the bottom of the scale. As Lady Townley puts it, " 'Tis good to have an universal taste; we should love wit, but for variety be able to divert ourselves with the extravagance of those who want [lack] it." The company of "young, idle people" who frequent Lady Townley's house divert themselves with Sir Fopling's extravagancies: his ignorance, his pretentious airs, his bad French, and his ultra-modish finery.

Among the women, Lady Townley, who loves wit, and Lady Woodville, Harriet's old-fashioned mother, who fears it — especially as personified by Dorimant, "the prince of all the devils in town" who "delights in nothing but rapes and riots" — are outside the scale. The label names of these two older ladies place them in obvious opposition: town versus country. Harriet, "wild, witty, lovesome, beautiful and young," is a brilliant example of the emancipated lady who wields her weapons skillfully in the eternal war between the sexes. She loves Dorimant, but she will never let him guess how much. The guarded wit combats between the two are waged with double meanings and polite insults. Thus, in the following passage, *play* equals both gambling and wenching.

DORIMANT. You were talking of play, madam. Pray, what may be your stint?

HARRIET. A little harmless discourse in public walks, or at most an appointment in a box, bare-faced, at the playhouse. You are for masks and private meetings, where women engage for all they are worth, I hear.

DORIMANT. I have been used to deep play, but I can make one at small game when I like my gamester well.

HARRIET. And be so unconcerned you'll ha' no pleasure in 't.

DORIMANT. Where there is a considerable sum to be won, the hope of drawing people in makes every trifle considerable.

HARRIET. The sordidness of men's natures, I know, makes 'em willing to flatter and comply with the rich, though they are sure never to be the better for 'em.

DORIMANT. 'Tis in their power to do us good, and we despair not but at some time or other they may be willing.

HARRIET. To men who have fared in this town like you, 'twould be a great mortification to live on hope. Could you keep a Lent for a mistress?

DORIMANT. In expectation of a happy Easter and, though time be very precious, think forty days well lost to gain your favor.

HARRIET. Mr. Bellair, let us walk; 'tis time to leave him. Men grow dull when they begin to be particular.

DORIMANT. You're mistaken; flattery will not ensue, though I know you're greedy of the praises of the whole Mall.

HARRIET. You do me wrong.

DORIMANT. I do not. As I followed you, I observed how you were pleased when the fops cried, "She's handsome — very handsome! By God, she is!" and whispered aloud your name. The thousand several forms you put your face into, then, to make yourself more agreeable! How wantonly you played with your head, flung back your locks, and looked smilingly over your shoulder at 'em!

HARRIET. I do not go begging the men's, as you do the ladies', good liking, with a sly softness in your looks and a gentle slowness in your bows as you pass 'em — as thus, sir. (*Acts him.*) Is not this like you?

Harriet keeps her ascendancy over Dorimant by maintaining her scornful, sophisticated pose. Eventually he breaks down, confesses his love, and offers, "I will renounce all the joy I have in friendship and wine, sacrifice to you all the interest I have in other women — " "Hold!" cries Harriet; "Though I wish you devout, I would not have you turn fanatic." But when she is sure that she has Dorimant fast in her toils, Harriet takes her moment of triumph, saying brutally to Mrs. Loveit, "Mr. Dorimant has been your god almighty long enough; 'tis time to think of another." Like Dorimant, Harriet is witty, well-bred, and "strangely ill-natured."

It is a mistake to think of Dorimant as a rake reformed by the love of a good woman. He shows no signs of reformation, and we may conjecture that after a few months of married bliss he will return to his old courses — perhaps even to Bellinda and Mrs. Loveit. Moreover, Harriet is not (except in the sense that she still has her virginity) a *good* woman. She declares that she will never do anything "against the rules of decency and honor," but within those elastic rules she can be as calculating and unscrupulous as Dorimant. Dorimant is a rake captured (at least temporarily) by a very clever woman, who uses her natural weapons to secure for herself the husband of her choice, a place in society, and residence in London — "this dear town," which Harriet loves so much that she "can scarce endure the country in landscapes and hangings."

Emilia and Bellinda are lesser libertine wits, still unfinished. Emilia is beautful, modest, and unaffected, but too conventionally virtuous. Dorimant has tried her virtue without success and believes that only a husband can corrupt her. "I have known many a woman make a difficulty of losing a maidenhead, who have afterwards made none of making a cuckold." Bellinda surrenders her virtue to Dorimant, but she is unwise enough to believe the extravagant promises that men make in love. Still, under Dorimant's tutelage, she may mature in judgment and in time "come to keep her coach and pay parish duties [as a kept mistress] if the good humor of the age continue." But there is no hope for Mrs. Loveit, who is too emotional, too passionate in her love and jealousy, ever to be a wit. Passion is folly, the antithesis of wit. Comedy laughs at it.

As for Etherege's style, Captain Radcliffe was right; it is "superfine, with words correct in every line." Etherege maintains his characters as much by the quality of their speeches as by the substance. His true wits talk in sharp, precise, often balanced or periodic, sentences, wasting no words and rarely using the commonplace, interjections of ordinary speech: *well, well then, what, how, come, pshaw, faith, Gad, Lord, by the world, odso,* and the like. Old Bellair rambles, and lards his discourse with such old-fashioned mechanical phrases as *a dod, mum, out a pize,* and *a pize on 'em.* Sir Fopling's speeches are trivial, aimless, and appropriate to his ignorance and conceit.

And, of course, Mrs. Loveit uses all too often the language of passion: "devil — monster — barbarian . . . plague, war, famine, fire! — Lightning blast him!" In urbane, sophisticated comedy, passionate speeches are ridiculous.

To the enthusiast in wit every page of *The Man of Mode* is sheer delight. But man does not live by head alone; the heart, too, has its functions. Admiration is all very well, but in any age playgoers seek to identify themselves with the protagonists of a comedy — no easy matter with such airy, brittle people as Dorimant and Harriet. Truly great comedy engages the emotions as well as the minds of its audience.

Every Restoration poet aspired to comic wit, and a few achieved it, usually, however, mixed with intrigue and humor (or satire) in a palatable blend. Dryden, for example, showed his fancy and judgment to good effect in the delightful subplots of *Secret Love* (1667), *Marriage à la Mode* (1672), and *Amphitryon* (1690). Wycherley showed off his labored wit in *The Gentleman Dancing Master* (1672) and (mixed with satire) in *The Country Wife* (1675). Other witty comedies worth listing are Crowne's *Sir Courtly Nice* (1685), Rawlins' *Tunbridge-Wells* (1678), Sedley's *Bellamira* (1687), Mountfort's *Greenwich Park* (1691), and Vanbrugh's *The Provoked Wife* (1697). But the mantle of Etherege fell on William Congreve's shoulders. It was Congreve's misfortune to reach his artistic maturity at a time when the Town was losing its taste for wit, and *The Way of the World* (1700), one of the best wit comedies in the English language, had (according to Dryden) "but moderate success" on the stage, "though it deserved much better." Certainly it had a magnificent production and an all-star cast, with wild Jack Verbruggen as Mirabell, Thomas Betterton as Fainall, beautiful Anne Bracegirdle as Millamant, Elizabeth Barry as Mrs. Marwood, and the delightful comedienne Elinor Leigh as Lady Wishfort.

William Congreve was born in Yorkshire and educated at Kilkenny School and Trinity College in Ireland, and at the Middle Temple in London. His learning and genial good manners brought him the friendship of Dryden, Southerne, Gildon, Walsh, and other literary lights who shone daily at Will's Coffee-house, the rendezvous of the wits. Early attracted to writing as a profession, by 1700 Congreve was famous as a translator and as the author of a novel, three popular comedies, and a successful "tragedy" with a happy ending. He moved in the best social circles; he was a shareholder in the Betterton-Barry-Bracegirdle company at Lincoln's Inn Fields; and he was in love with Anne Bracegirdle, "the virgin actress," who was the model for his heroines.

Unfortunately, Congreve was too much a wit to be content with pandering to popular taste. In his dedication prefixed to *The Way of the World*, he declared that very little of the play "was prepared for that general taste which seems now to be predominant in the palates of our audience." The end-of-the-century, largely middle-class audience had little appetite for his sophisticated comedy and lacked the mental agility to keep up with the rapid play of his wit. Perhaps the reaction of one playgoer is typical of the majority. A few days after the first performance of the play, a Warwickshire visitor in London, Mary, Lady Marrow, wrote to a friend, "'The Way of the World,' Congreve's new play, doth not answer expectations, there being no plot in it but many witty things to ridicule the Chocolate House and the fantastical part of the world."

Dear Lady Marrow — what, no plot? The fact is that there is so much plot that often modern readers (and even some critics) become confused and lose their way. But Congreve submerged his fable under the flow of his witty dialogue; he developed his plot so casually that to a hasty reader or an inattentive listener the play seems to be merely a collage of clever conversations. Nevertheless, there is a plot, but, as Thomas Davies remarked, in *Dramatic Miscellanies* (1784), it is "singularly intricate."

"The way of the world," a catch phrase used cynically by Fainall and mockingly by Mirabell, is the blend of behavior patterns approved by polite society at the end of the seventeenth century. The wits in the comedy are all busily engaged in outwitting each other. To get Millamant's hand in marriage, Mirabell, the top wit and fine gentleman of the play, has to deceive and defeat Lady Wishfort, Millamant's aunt. It seems that at his death Sir Jonathan Wishfort, Millamant's foolish uncle, left her six thousand pounds outright and another six thousand if she married in accordance with her aunt's wishes. Lady Wishfort abominates Mirabell and wants Millamant to marry her country cousin, Sir Wilfull Witwoud. But Millamant detests Sir Wilfull and, although she hates to admit the fact, loves Mirabell.

Earlier Mirabell had pretended love for Lady Wishfort to cover up his wooing of Millamant. With that plot exposed and defeated, he plans now to pass off his servant, Waitwell, as a fictitious rich uncle, Sir Rowland, and to set him a-wooing Lady Wishfort, who, "full of the vigor of fifty-five," would "marry anything that resembled a man, though 'twere no more than what a butler could pinch out of a napkin." Before matters go too far, Mirabell will disclose the cheat, threaten to make Lady Wishfort a laughingstock in the Town, and thus blackmail her into giving her consent to his marriage with Millamant. To guarantee against a double-cross, Mirabell marries Waitwell to Foible, Lady Wishfort's maid. His plot is neither gallant nor honorable, but it is all in "the way of the world." And six thousand pounds was a very large sum.

Mirabell and Millamant, two good-natured wits, are the ideal people of the comedy. Mirabell (an experienced amorist, but now too besottedly in love with Millamant to care for fun and games) is amiable, far-sighted, prudent, learned, witty, and worldly-wise. ("Mirabell, the fine gentleman of the play," said Thomas Davies, "is, I believe, not very distant from the real character of Congreve.") Mirabell is sententious, a maker of cynical maxims: "A woman who is not a fool can have but one reason for associating with a man who is one." "Beauty is the lover's gift. 'Tis he bestows your charms." "For sure, to please a fool is some degree of folly." "Errors which love produces have ever been accounted venial." Unlike Dorimant, Mirabell has moral scruples; for instance, his "virtue" kept him from trying "downright personally to debauch" Lady Wishfort, who fairly panted to be debauched. In his wit combats with Millamant, Mirabell usually comes off second best because he is serious and she is flippant. After one skirmish he soliloquizes, "A fellow that lives in a windmill has not a more whimsical dwelling than the heart of a man that is lodged in a woman. . . . To know this, and yet continue to be in love is to be made wise from the dictates of reason, and yet persevere to play the fool by the force of instinct."

Millamant is one of the most delightful heroines in all English comedy. She hides wisdom, tenderness, and love beneath a fanciful mask of coquetry and affection. In the famous "proviso" scene — a stock comic device carried out to its highest power — Millamant's wisdom shines through her whimsical language as she lays down the conditions under which she may consent at last to "dwindle" into a wife. "Good Mirabell, don't let us be familiar or fond, nor kiss before folks, like my Lady Fadler and Sir Francis, nor go to Hyde Park together the first Sunday in a new chariot to provoke eyes and whispers, and then never be seen there together again, as if we were proud of one another the first week and ashamed of one another ever after. Let us never visit together nor go to a play together, but let us be very strange and well-bred. Let us be as strange as if we had been married a great while, and as well-bred as if we were not married at all." To this brilliant gambit, Mirabell can retort only with provisos showing his concern for his reputation as a husband and for the welfare of his future son — whose birth may be presumed, he suggests, "with a blessing on our endeavors." With an arch look and a tone of pretended horror, Millamant replies, "Odious endeavors!" Adorable Millamant!

Opposed to Mirabell and Millamant are Fainall and Mrs. Marwood, two ingenious wits who are engaged in a deception of their own. Socially and intellectually, they differ little from the top wits, but they are passionate and ill-natured, and we are advised not to like them. (Unfortunately, most of us are ill-natured too, and we find it hard to dislike them.) Mrs. Marwood (who is unmarried) is Fainall's mistress; indeed she was his mistress long before Fainall married Lady Wishfort's daughter, Arabella Languish, a rich young widow. Moved by jealousy of Millamant — she herself had "a month's mind" to Mirabell — Mrs. Marwood exposed Mirabell's pretended passion for Lady Wishfort, and thus became "the officious obstacle" to Mirabell's match with Millamant. Fainall, aware of Mrs. Marwood's penchant, is jealous of Mirabell.

At the beginning of the play, Fainall, who would be a bankrupt without his wife's money, is not aware that he has already been outwitted. Before Mirabell fell in love with Millamant, he had an affair with Arabella, who, as a widow (according to the myth of the times), was wanton and inflammable. Fearing a possible biological consequence of their love, Mirabell arranged for his mistress to marry Fainall, "a man lavish of his morals, an interested and professing friend, a false and designing lover, yet one whose wit and outward fair behavior have gained a reputation with the Town enough to make that woman stand excused who has suffered herself to be won by his addresses." The "consequence" never materialized. In the course of the play, Mrs. Fainall, a good-natured wit who detests her husband, asks Mirabell, "Why did you make me marry this man?" Mirabell explains, apologetically, "To save that idol, reputation. . . . A better man ought not to have been sacrificed to the occasion, a worse had not answered the purpose."

We must not ask why Mirabell failed to marry Arabella himself; 'twas the way of the Restoration world. A gentleman never thought of marrying his mistress, nor did she expect him to make her an honest woman. His choice for a wife must be a lady of unquestioned virtue. But Mirabell showed a serious concern for Arabella's reputation and took the legal steps necessary to assure her future. Arabella's complaint is not that he talked her into marrying another, but that he chose Fainall to be the gull. It was the way of the world also that Fainall should marry Arabella "to make lawful prize of a rich widow's wealth" and spend it on his mistress, Mrs. Marwood. Fainall returns his wife's hatred with interest, and would gladly see her dead.

As the play opens, Fainall and Mrs. Marwood are carrying on their affair under Mrs. Fainall's nose — even in Lady Wishfort's house. They would like to outwit the entire Wishfort family, get possession of that part of Mrs. Fainall's fortune not yet deeded to Fainall, and get control of Lady Wishfort's estate. Although they are greedy and malicious, they are wits, not villains. In Fainall's own phrase, their deceits are "all in the way of the world."

Of course a Restoration comedy must have a complement of fools and humorists as whetstones for the wits. Witwoud and Petulant, half-hearted suitors for Millamant's hand, are made to appear ridiculous, "not so much," said Congreve, "through a natural folly (which is incorrigible and therefore not proper for the stage) as through an affected wit, which at the same time that it is affected is also false." Witwoud believes that levity is the soul of wit and tries to pass off shop-worn similitudes as brand-new wares. He is "a fool with a good memory and some few scraps of other folks' wit." He lacks wit "as often as his memory fails him and his commonplace of comparisons." Vain, boorish Petulant thinks that wit lies in impudence, insolence, and bad manners. He has a freakish turn of fancy but not a scrap of judgment. Unfortunately, Congreve drew his fools so deftly that they passed with his audience for Truewits. The play, he said, "had been acted two or three days" before some of the hasty judges in the audience "could find the leisure to distinguish between the character of a Witwoud and a Truewit." Probably, by her "fantastical part of the world," Lady Marrow meant Petulant and Witwoud.

Lady Wishfort (whose name, of course, should be read as Wishfor't) is the most fully developed character in the comedy. She is a foolish old woman, desperately eager to recapture the carnal delights of youth. The evidence in the play suggests that she has a citizen background and is the widow of a City knight. She is coarsely vituperative on occasion, and can rail like a fishwife at her servants. Yet she is also a Puritan. She tells us that she brought up her daughter averse "to the very sight of men" and made her listen to long lectures against "singing and dancing and such debaucheries, and going to filthy plays and profane music-meetings, where the lewd trebles squeak nothing but bawdy, and the basses roar blasphemy." Her daughter, she says, "would have swooned at the sight or name of an obscene play-book!" On the mantelpiece in her dressing room Lady Wishfort has Quarles's *Divine Emblems,* Prynne's *Historio-Mastix* (an early attack on the stage), Collier's *Short View of the Immorality and Profaneness of the English Stage,* and Bunyan's works.

Because she is unsure of herself and her position in society — even her mechanical phrase, "As I'm a person," suggests her uncertainty — she is constantly worried about decorum and "that idol, reputation." She is governed by emotion. Although she hates Mirabell so much that in his absence she would gladly hire a villain to assassinate him, in his presence the embers of love smoldering in her withered breast flame up again. Wooed by the false Sir Rowland, she tries to mask her eagerness with language so affectedly pompous that it sounds like Mrs. Malaprop's "nice derangement of epitaphs." — "Well, Sir Rowland, you have the way — you are no novice in the labyrinth of love; you have the clue. But as I am a person, Sir Rowland, you must not attribute my yielding to any sinister appetite or indigestion of widowhood; nor impute my complacency to any lethargy of continence. I hope you do not think me prone to any iteration of nuptials — If you do, I protest I must recede — or think that I have made a prostitution of decorums; but in the vehemence of compassion, and to save the life of a person of so much importance —" It is ironic that Lady Wishfort should have the best line in the play: "Ah, dear Marwood, what's integrity to an opportunity?"

Lady Wishfort's country nephew, Sir Wilfull Witwoud, is "an odd mixture of bashfulness and obstinacy — But when he's drunk he's as loving as the monster [Caliban] in *The Tempest.*"

At the age of forty he decides to travel and see the world. Unkind Millamant calls him a "superannuated lubber," but he is merely an honest bumpkin who reeks of stable reality and is set up in contrast to the two fantastics, Witwoud (his half-brother) and Petulant.

The simple device of an overheard conversation gives Mrs. Marwood not only the outline of Mirabell's plot against Lady Wishfort but also the facts about Mrs. Fainall's premarital affair with Mirabell. When he learns about the latter, Fainall is furious. "I, it seems, am a husband, a rank husband, and my wife a very errant, rank wife — all in the way of the world. 'Sdeath, to be an anticipated cuckold, a cuckold in embryo! Sure, I was born with budding antlers, like a young satyr or a citizen's child. 'Sdeath! to be outwitted, to be out-jilted — out-matrimony'd! — If I had kept my speed like a stag, 'twere somewhat — but to crawl after with my horns like a snail, and be out-stripped by my wife — 'tis scurvy wedlock."

Mrs. Marwood urges him to make good use of her information, and he agrees. But first he has to think over the situation. Resorting to witty sophistry, he concludes that since he never loved his wife he can't be jealous. As for his reputation —

> I married not for it, so that's out of the question; and as to my part in my wife's — why, she had parted with hers before; so bringing none to me, she can take none from me. 'Tis against all rule of play that I should lose to one who has not wherewithal to stake.
>
> MRS. MARWOOD. Besides, you forget marriage is honorable.
>
> FAINAL. Hum, faith, and that's well thought on. Marriage is honorable, as you say, and if so, wherefore should cuckoldom be a discredit, being derived from so honorable a root?

Intent on tipping his horns with gold, Fainall joins his mistress in a counterplot. Mrs. Marwood, who poses as Lady Wishfort's best friend, unmasks Waitwell as the false Sir Rowland and exposes Mirabell's scheme. Then, making great play with the discovery of his wife's earlier affair with Mirabell,

Fainall presents his demands: Mrs. Fainall must make over to him the title to the remainder of her fortune; Lady Wishfort must give him Millamant's six thousand pounds, which, he argues, Millamant has forfeited by refusing to marry Sir Wilfull; and Lady Wishfort must submit her own estate to his management and oblige herself never to marry. Unless his demands are met, Fainall will sue for a divorce, exposing Mrs. Fainall's reputation to the lewdness of the law courts and the pollution of the public press.

Lady Wishfort is helpless. Even the exposure of Fainall's affair with Mrs. Marwood (the maids had once caught them *in flagrante*) and Millamant's desperate agreement to marry Sir Wilfull (who doesn't really want her) have no effect on Fainall, who refuses to moderate his demands. But cautious Mirabell has an ace in the hole. With a triumphant flourish he produces "A deed of conveyance of the whole estate real of Arabella Languish, widow, in trust to Edward Mirabell," a deed executed before Arabella married Fainall. Because this document predates the deed in Fainall's possession, by which he has acquired half of his wife's estate, Fainall is suddenly penniless, and his threats are empty. Fainall and Marwood, outwitted and discomfited, slink off the stage, vowing vengeance. Mirabell gets his Millamant and six thousand pounds; Lady Wishfort forgives everybody in sight; and the game ends in a light-hearted dance — all in the way of the world.

The Way of the World is critical comedy; its dramatis personae is neatly divisible into the Witwouds and the Truewits. But there are two groups of Truewits, one well-intentioned and one malicious. The standard of judgment is no longer that of *The Man of Mode* — the possession of *libertine* wit. Dorimant and Harriet, witty but unscrupulous, have become Fainall and Marwood, who are rejected because of the very qualities which would have made them the top wits of the coterie a generation earlier. The coterie has gone, taking its standards along into limbo. Mirabell and Millamant, the new top wits, are as clever in their ways as Dorimant and Harriet, but they are good-natured, and they cling to a few principles of decency and honor.

However, the wheel has not yet come full circle; the — perhaps ironically — approved wits, Mirabell, Millamant, and Mrs. Fainall, have more sensibility, or humanity, than their prototypes in earlier wit comedy, but they are by no means patterns of virtue. Although their way of life is superior to that of Fainall and Mrs. Marwood, they are not above employing deceit and trickery to gain the ends which, in their eyes, justify the means.

The Way of the World is much more than an intricate plot and a sparkling exhibition of witty dialogue. Beneath Congreve's irony lie tenderness and understanding — even for the fools and the malicious wits. Although his characters play heartless, worldly games and banter with the polished cynicism of true sophisticates, they remain struggling human beings who, like all of us, have to worry about money, fight to keep up appearances, and bow to "that idol, reputation." Congreve contemplates the ways of his world judiciously, meting out rewards and punishments according to the deserts of his characters, but he expects us to be tolerant of their faults and amused, as he is, by their foibles. Although the malicious wits threaten revenge as they leave the stage, the comedy ends on a note of reconciliation: we are led to believe that even Fainall and his wife may be brought together to rub along in frigid amity. Compromise, too, is the way of the world.

*** 15 ***

The Comedy of Tears

IN THE LAST DECADE of the century, a sensitive playgoer would have been aware of a steadily increasing interest in dramatic morality, especially among the ladies in the audience. He would have noted, too, how tearfully the audience reacted to a few tentative scenes showing the reformation of a rake by the power of a good woman. At the same time he would have seen only a little lessening of the masculine taste for eroticism, seduction, and cuckoldry. Anti-morality was still strong, but the forces of conventional morality were massing for war.

It was time for a change. The popular Restoration plots were wearing thin, and playwrights, desperate for novelty — especially after 1695, when two companies were competing for patronage — were turning to all kinds of outlandish themes and devices. The tragic poets plumped for sensationalism, rape, incest, and adultery, setting their plays in countries remote in time and place: Persia, Turkey, Surinam, Sardinia, Parthia, Lacedemonia, Troy, Egypt, and Siam. Their characters and plots were as outlandish as their settings. For example, in *The Unnatural Mother* (1697), Cemat, a wicked Siamese, tries to rape his own sister, Chousera. Caught in time and frustrated by his mother, he stabs Chousera fatally. Then Cemat dies from poison administered earlier by his mother, equally wicked Callipia. At the end of the play, Callipia, who is to be burned at the stake for her many crimes, runs mad, stabs a priest, and kills herself. Even wilder is the anonymous *The Fatal Discovery* (1698), from which we learn that years before the events of the play, a young man, Cornaro, had slept with his mother, Berengaria, believing her to be a housemaid. (Berengaria, posing as a mistress, thought she was entertaining her estranged husband.) At the opening of the play, the result of this incestuous union, Eromena, is of marriageable age. Cornaro, returning after fifteen years abroad, falls in love with Eromena and marries her. Then, too late, he discovers that his wife is also his daughter and his half-sister. Of course the three principals die with appropriate violence.

In the 1690s the comic writers, too, were avidly searching for variety and change. The best comic writers of the early Restoration had died or had given up writing for the stage. Ravenscroft, D'Urfey, Settle, and Tate were still grinding out farces, and Congreve, Cibber, Farquhar, and Vanbrugh were testing their pens, but the bulk of the comic fare was sorry stuff written by miserable hacks and amateurs. Even John Dryden could produce, as his valedictory play, only *Love Triumphant* (1694), a woefully poor tragicomedy, which "was damned by the universal cry of the Town."

Eager to attract audiences, the comic poets piled on the complications of plot and tried every farcical device they could invent. Henry Higden, for instance, introduced a number of rowdy drinking scenes into his *The Wary Widow* (1693). Onstage the players drank so much wine that they were "completely drunk before the end of the third act, and being therefore unable to proceed . . . they very properly dismissed the audience." Other comic poets stressed eroticism and adultery, wrote bawdy epilogues to be spoken by actresses in breeches, and dirty songs to be sung by little girls, and never missed a chance for a smirking allusion to the apparently growing taste for homosexuality among the beaux. Farce and fornication ruled the comic stage.

With the decadence of drama came an increased demand for operas, which often cost the companies more than they could afford. It is said that Settle's *The Fairy Queen* (1692) — *A Midsummer Night's Dream* made into a musical nightmare — cost three thousand pounds for clothes, scenes, and music. The actors imported French dancers and Italian singers at incredible cost: they paid the dancer Balon four hundred guineas for five weeks' work, and the eunuch Francisco Senesinon a hundred and twenty guineas for a mere five performances.

There were external, as well as internal, forces at work to change and moralize the stage, even before Collier's sweeping condemnation of the drama in 1698. Since the early days of the Restoration, Parliament had passed scores of puritanical laws, most of which were consistently ignored by evildoers, watchmen, bailiffs, and magistrates. But in the last decade of the century, societies for the reformation of manners multiplied like rabbits all over England. Composed of rigid pietists, these societies insisted on the enforcement of all "blue" laws and informed against lawbreakers. They pounced upon every hint of profanity or immorality on the stage and sought ultimately the suppression of the theaters. In *A Sermon Preached to the Societies for the Reformation of Manners in London and Westminster* (1700), Timothy Rogers, M.A., indicted the stage "as the great cause of immorality." "And indeed," he said, "from thence a huge stream of vice comes flowing down upon us. And till that impure fountain is stopped, there can be no thorough reformation, no more than any cure of a disease whilst the main cause remains."

The societies found an ally in King William III, a cold, morose man who, whatever his private sins, gave a public example of marital fidelity. He issued frequent proclamations against debauchery and commanded all law officers to execute the laws against "blasphemy, profane swearing and cursing, drunkenness, lewdness," etc. He had no use for the theaters, but at his behest various Lord Chamberlains sent forth warnings to the actors against anything in a play which was not "strictly agreeable to religion and good manners." Moreover the London grand juries and the Middlesex justices "presented" the theaters as nuisances and as "nurseries of debauchery and blasphemy." They brought charges against Congreve for writing *The Double Dealer* (1693) and D'Urfey for writing *Don Quixote* (1694), and against Tonson and Briscoe, the booksellers, for printing such obscene plays. Informers brought about the arrest of several players for "using very profane words upon the stage," and the London grand jury even tried to prohibit the posting of play-bills about the city, arguing that the bills encouraged "vice and profaneness."

Jeremy Collier's *A Short View of the Immorality and Profaneness of the English Stage* (1698) brought the external attack upon the stage to a climax. Collier's declared purpose was to display in detail the sins of the modern poets, "their smuttiness of expression; their swearing, profaneness, and lewd application of scripture; their abuse of the clergy; their making their top characters libertines, and giving them success in their debauchery." Collier assumed as the premise of his strictures that all pleasure was evil and that the pleasure of plays was the worst of evils. He ranged at large through Restoration drama (chiefly comedy), pointing out trivialities, mistaking badinage for profanity, and seeing smut where none was intended. But on the whole he cited enough foul examples to satisfy his fellow pharisees and to stir up the forces of morality to further attacks. The better poets struck back at their persecutors, ridiculed and reviled Collier, and proclaimed their own virtuous intentions and reformatory purposes.

But the strongest pressure for change came from the audience itself. It had lost the support and leadership of a libertine King and Court, and its sense of solidarity as a coterie. It had been infiltrated by ladies who loved to linger over tender sentiments and by respectable middle-class tradesmen and their wives, whose views were conventionally moral. The merchants who had grown rich in "the City" and now sought diversion and social acceptance in "the Town" disliked wit and satire — especially at their expense — and had no taste for high tragedy and the spiritual sufferings of a noble soul. They liked farce, and they wanted emotional excitement, not intellectual stimulus. They enjoyed the novelty of morality on the stage and wallowed in the luxury of tears.

In the 1690s, then, the audience was moving steadily toward sentimentalism: the emotion-supported belief that this is the best of all possible worlds, that there is good in everyone, and that a sinner can be reformed by appeals to his sensibility — often miscalled his "reason." Sentimentalism is a common human attitude, the antithesis of negative cynicism, and, because it is affirmative and acquiescent, more durable than cynicism. The wonder is, not that sentimentalism trickled into late seventeenth-century drama (swamping the stage with tears in the next century), but that Restoration cynicism lasted as long as it did. The pendulum swung back from cynicism to sentimentalism, from license and lubricity to decorum and decency, from anti-morality to conventional morality.

The change did not come overnight, of course. There were hints of the new sentimentalism in the comedies of the mid-1680s, foreshadowings which became steadily clearer in the next decade. In 1695 Colley Cibber, a promising young actor at the Theater Royal, turned poet (he said) out of necessity; the company paid him only thirty shillings a week and refused to cast him in leading parts. He decided, therefore, to write a comedy with a major role tailored to fit his own comic style. Well aware of the slowly changing tastes of his audience, he seems to have decided to please both the moralists and the anti-moralists, to eat his cake and have it too. The resulting sex-intrigue comedy, *Love's Last Shift, or The Fool in Fashion* (January, 1696), which reversed the conventional anti-marriage theme, was a great success.

For himself Cibber created the role of a coxcomb, Sir Novelty Fashion, in the long-established tradition of Etherege's Sir Fopling

Flutter. For his main plot he developed the character of Loveless, a typical Restoration rakehell, who had married Amanda, "a woman of strict virtue," had wasted his substance in riotous living, and, eight years before the events of the play, had fled abroad to escape his creditors. During his absence he was told that Amanda had died. As the comedy opens, Loveless has just returned to England. He is penniless, happy-go-lucky, and unrepentant. He does not know that Amanda is alive and as beautiful as ever, even after an attack of smallpox which has changed her appearance. She is equipped with a newly inherited fortune worth two thousand pounds a year; she still loves the prodigal, and she yearns to reclaim and reform him.

Following the advice of a friend, she sets a trap for Loveless. A servant, pretending to mistake him for another, brings him to Amanda's lodgings late at night, as to an assignation with a mistress. Amanda, "loosely dressed" and lusciously tempting, pretends that she does not know him and puts on a show of indignation, but finally she yields to the passionate lovemaking of Loveless, who, of course, does not recognize her. Loveless accomplishes the remarkable feat of cuckolding himself.

The next morning Amanda tells Loveless that she is his wife; as proof she shows his name tattooed on her arm. Loveless is confused, confounded, and stricken with remorse. Suddenly the fundamental goodness which (according to the sentimentalists) is in all men wells up and bubbles over in sudsy, iambic prose. "Oh," he cries, "thou hast roused me from my deep lethargy of vice! For hitherto my soul has been enslaved to loose desires, to vain deluding follies, and shadows of substantial bliss; but now I wake with joy to find my rapture real. Thus let me kneel and pay my thanks to her whose conquering virtue has at last subdued me. Here will I fix, thus prostrate, sigh my shame, and wash my crimes in never-ceasing tears of penitence." Amanda accepts his reformation with lachrymose joy, but Loveless has not finished. All his life he has accepted the fashionable anti-marriage cliché and has scorned the very name of "wife." Now he has learned that a wife can be "charming beyond the wishes of luxuriant love." "Is it then a name, a word," he asks, "shall rob thee of thy worth? Can fancy be a surer guide to happiness than reason? Oh, I have wandered like a benighted wretch, and lost myself in life's unpleasing journey!

> 'Twas heedless fancy first that made me stray,
> But reason now breaks forth and lights me on my way."

At this point, husband and wife go off-stage hand in hand, into the dawn of a glorious new day.

In his epilogue, Cibber deemed it wise to apologize to the libertines in his audience:

> Now, sirs, to you whose sole religion's drinking,
> Whoring, roaring, without the pain of thinking,
> He fears he's made a fault you'll ne'er forgive,
> A crime beyond the hopes of a reprieve.
> An honest rake forgo the joys of life,
> His whores and wine, t' embrace a dull chaste wife!
> Such out-of-fashion stuff! But then again,
> He's lewd for above four acts, gentlemen. . . .
> Four acts for your coarse palates was designed,
> But then the ladies' taste is more refined;
> They, for Amanda's sake, will sure be kind.

Cibber's variation on the usual theme of intrigue comedy was not the mere fact of Loveless's reformation. In romantic comedy, from the time of the Elizabethans, rakes and rascals who performed a volte-face at the end of a play were common enough — see, for instance, wicked Oliver in *As You Like It.* The novelty was in part the depiction of a truly virtuous wife, but even more the treatment of Loveless's reformation: the dramatic preparation which made it an obligatory scene, and the unrealistic dwelling upon the rake's repentance and his wife's happiness at the salvation of a sinner. According to Tom Davies, "The joy of unexpected reconcilement, from Loveless's remorse and penitence, spread such an uncommon rapture of pleasure in the audience, that never were spectators more happy in easing their minds by uncommon and repeated plaudits. The honest tears shed by the audience at this interview conveyed a strong reproach to our licentious poets, and was to Cibber the highest mark of honor." The sophisticated early-Restoration coterie would have laughed Cibber's play to death; the end-of-the-century audience loved it.

But there were still a few die-hards. As the story goes, Captain John Vanbrugh saw a performance of *Love's Last Shift* and was so amused at the notion of a rakehell reforming permanently that in six weeks he wrote a farce-intrigue sequel, calling it *The Relapse, or Virtue in Danger* (December, 1696). His purpose was to show that Loveless's newly acquired virtue was unstable. Vanbrugh's Loveless succumbs to the charms of Amanda's cousin, Berinthia, a beautiful young widow. In a climactic scene Loveless picks up Berinthia and carries her off to a bedroom, while she cries "(*Very softly*) Help! Help!" But Vanbrugh could do nothing with the original Amanda, whose virtue is so overpowering that Young Worthy, defeated in his attempt to seduce her, finds his lust turned to sentimental adoration.

Cibber was delighted with *The Relapse*. In his *Apology* (1740) he wrote that Captain Vanbrugh "not only did me honor as an author by writing his *Relapse* as a sequel or second part to *Love's Last Shift,* but as an actor, too, by preferring me to the chief character of his own play, which . . . he had ennobled by the style of Baron of Foppington." Cibber had no moral convictions. Like a growing number of his contemporaries — notably Farquhar, Burnaby, and Mrs. Centlivre — he adopted the new devices of sentimentalism only because he saw that his audience liked them.

The success of Cibber's first play so encouraged him that in the next eight years, while acting steadily, he turned out seven more original plays or adaptations of older plays. His eighth play, *The Careless Husband* (1704), is perhaps his best; it is a good example of the new "genteel" comedy. In his prologue

Cibber argued that the persons appropriate to comedy are not those of low degree but

> they whose birth and education says
> They've every help that should improve mankind,
> Yet still live slaves to a vile tainted mind . . .
> Such are the persons we today provide,
> And Nature's fools for once are laid aside.

Accordingly, *The Careless Husband* deals with people of birth, breeding, and inherited wealth, who gossip, play cards, attend balls, dinners, and music-meetings, amuse themselves with flirtations and casual adulteries, and care very little for wit or wisdom. They are neither Truewits nor Witwouds.

The careless husband is Sir Charles Easy, a kindly, generous, lazy fellow, who married for money, is kind to his wife even though he does not love her, and has his affairs with other women as a matter of course. He is not truly a slave "to a vile tainted mind," but he has had (and is trying to end) an affair with Lady Graveairs, "a young, handsome, wild, well-jointured widow," who still loves him. Because he is too lazy to pursue ladies of quality, Sir Charles has his wife's maid, Mrs. Edging, as his domestic "convenient," for the ease of his body.

Lady Easy is a paragon of virtue. She loves her husband and is fully aware of his infidelities, but she is too generous and considerate of his feelings to scold him. She nurses her pain in silence, hoping that while Sir Charles's "humane nature is not quite shook off" he may reform. Lady Easy's friend, Lady Betty Modish, is a coquette who trifles cruelly with the affections of Lord Morelove, a man of sensibility, sincerity, and good breeding, and flirts dangerously with Lord Foppington (played by Cibber, of course), a dilettante libertine who believes that "the pleasure of a fine woman is like that of her virtue, not so much the thing as the reputation of having it."

The plots are trifling. Sir Charles instructs Lord Morelove how to gain an ascendancy over Lady Betty, only to have his infatuated pupil forget his lessons and lose another battle to the triumphant coquette. At last Sir Charles delivers a stern lecture which brings Lady Betty to a realization of her folly, and moves her to tearful repentance and a promise to marry Lord Morelove. Everybody is happy, even Lord Foppington, who has had designs on Lady Betty's virtue but is too well-mannered to be out of humor with a woman for refusing him.

The true climax of the play is the obligatory scene between Sir Charles and Lady Easy. Lady Easy, returning home unexpectedly, finds her maid and Sir Charles (without his periwig) companionably asleep in two easy chairs, after having been in bed together. Struck to the heart by the sight, but still a loving, considerate wife, Lady Easy puts her scarf over Sir Charles's shaven poll to keep him from catching cold. When Sir Charles awakes and finds the scarf on his head, he is stricken with remorse and with amazement at his wife's prudence and love. For the first time he sees himself as he is and realizes how he has mistreated his wife. "How mean a vice is lying!" he muses, "and how often have these empty pleasures lulled my honor and my conscience to a lethargy, while I grossly have abused her, poorly skulking behind a thousand falsehoods."

Brimful of good intentions, he seeks out his wife, and in long tender passages of cadenced prose the two come to an understanding. Sir Charles concludes his self-abasement by declaring, "Your wondrous conduct has waked me to a sense of your disquiet past, and resolution never to disturb it more." Lady Easy, who has the spirit of an oyster, replies, weeping, "Oh, my dear! distract me not with this excess of goodness."

> SIR CHARLES. Nay, praise me not, lest I reflect how little I have deserved it; I see you are in pain to give me this confusion. Come, I will not shock your softness by my untimely blush for what is past, but rather soothe you to a pleasure at my sense of joy for my recovered happiness to come. Give, then, to my new-born love what name you please; it cannot, shall not, be too kind. Oh, it cannot be too soft for what my soul swells up with emulation to deserve — Receive me, then, en-

tire at last, and take what yet no woman ever truly had, my conquered heart!

LADY EASY. Oh, the soft treasure! Oh, the dear reward of long-deserving love! Now I am blessed indeed to see you kind without th' expense of pain in being so, to make you mine with easiness. Thus, thus, to have you mine is something more than happiness, 'tis double life, and madness of abounding joy.

According to Tom Davies, "The success of this comedy raised [Cibber] very deservedly to a high rank among our dramatic writers. . . . So well did Cibber, though a professed libertine through life, understand the dignity of virtue, that no comic author has drawn more delightful and striking pictures of it." It takes a sinner to depict virtue; saints are too self-conscious.

Although genteel comedy employed many of the devices of sentimentalism, it stood between two worlds. As the tide of middle-class morality swelled still higher in the eighteenth century, comedy, which had once ridiculed the vices and follies of man, came more and more to display their distresses, thus usurping the function of tragedy. The conventions of Restoration comedy were ignored or reversed, and the hallmarks of the new sentimental comedy became purity, pathos, penitence, and poetic justice. Libertines appeared in comedy only to be frustrated, defeated, or reformed in showers of tears. Orphans, forlorn maidens, unhappy wives, pious sons, constant lovers, and virtuous men with broken fortunes paraded across the comic stage to give the tender-minded audiences their fill of benevolence, morality, and pathos. The "comic" poets agreed that the function of comedy was to give moral instruction by precept and example. By the application of poetic justice and appeals to "the secret care of Providence," they proved that they were on the side of the angels. Conventional morality won its long war with the comic spirit and drove it into short farces — afterpieces which brought gusts of laughter to dry up a stage sodden with sentimental tears. The wheel of morality had come full circle.

A Selected Bibliography

* * *

The following are useful studies of the history, ideas, and manners of the Restoration period: G. N. Clark, *The Later Stuarts, 1660–1714,* Oxford, rev. ed., 1940; Preserved Smith, *A History of Modern Culture,* Vol. II, The Enlightenment, New York, 1930–1934; Basil Willey, *The Seventeenth Century Background,* Cambridge, 1934; Louis I. Bredvold, *The Intellectual Milieu of John Dryden,* Ann Arbor, 1939; Arthur Bryant, *King Charles II,* London, 1931, and *The England of Charles II,* London, 1934; and Joseph Wood Krutch, *Comedy and Conscience after the Restoration,* New York, 1924.

The classic study of the drama and stage of the period is still Allardyce Nicoll's *Restoration Drama, 1660–1700,* fourth ed., Cambridge, 1952. For activities in the Interregnum and the early history of the theaters, see Leslie Hotson, *The Commonwealth and Restoration Stage,* Cambridge, Mass., 1928 (re-issued, New York, 1962). Montague Summers presented interesting details about admissions, advertisements audiences, costumes, and stage practices in *The Restoration Theater,* London, 1934, and discussed a number of major and minor dramatists in *The Playhouse of Pepys,* New York, 1935. For acting, actresses, and the history of the companies, see J. H. Wilson, *All the King's Ladies,* Chicago, 1958, and *Mr. Goodman, the Player,* Pittsburgh, 1964. Court drama is fully covered by Eleanore Boswell's *The Restoration Court Stage,* Cambridge, Mass. 1932. Still useful are W. J. Lawrence, *The Elizabethan Playhouse and Other Studies,* Second Series, Stratford, 1913, and Lily B. Campbell, *Scenes and Machines on the English Stage during the Renaissance,* Cambridge, 1932. For dates of production and publication see *The London Stage,* Part 1, edd. E. L. Avery, A. H. Scouten, and William Van Lennep, Carbondale, Illinois, 1965.

The Rev. Montague Summers edited (copiously, if not always wisely) the complete works of six major Restoration dramatists:

Aphra Behn, 6 vols., London, 1915; William Congreve, 4 vols., London, 1923; William Wycherley, 4 vols., London, 1924; Thomas Otway, 3 vols., London, 1926; Thomas Shadwell, 5 vols., London, 1927; and John Dryden, 6 vols., London, 1931–1932. He edited also Buckingham's *The Rehearsal,* Stratford, 1914; a collection of *Restoration Comedies,* London, 1921, which includes Ravenscroft's *The London Cuckolds;* and *Shakespeare Adaptations,* Boston, 1922, which includes Duffett's *The Mock-Tempest.* A better edition of Otway is that by J. C. Ghosh, 2 vols., Oxford, 1932. The standard edition of Dryden is still the *Complete Works,* edd. Scott-Saintsbury, 18 vols., London, 1882–1883. Two volumes of a new *Works* of Dryden have appeared; Vol. VIII, edd. Dougald MacMillan and J. H. Smith, Berkeley, Cal., 1962, contains three of Dryden's earliest plays. Dryden's essays have been ably edited by George Watson in *Of Dramatic Poesy and Other Critical Essays,* 2 vols. (Everyman), London, 1962.

For Etherege see the sketchy edition of his *Dramatic Works,* ed. H. F. B. Brett-Smith, 2 vols., London, 1927. For Farquhar see the *Complete Works,* ed. Charles Stonehill, London, 1930. Lee's plays have been edited by Thomas B. Stroup and Arthur L. Cooke, 2 vols., New Brunswick, N. J., 1954–1955. Lee's *The Rival Queens* and Cibber's *Love's Last Shift* appear in *Plays of the Restoration and Eighteenth Century,* edd. Dougald MacMillan and Howard Mumford Jones, New York, 1931. Cibber's *The Careless Husband* and the first part of Dryden's *The Conquest of Granada* appear in *British Dramatists from Dryden to Sheridan,* edd. George H. Nettleton and Arthur E. Case, Boston, 1939. For smaller anthologies of Restoration plays see *Twelve Famous Plays of the Restoration and Eighteenth Century,* ed. Cecil A. Moore, New York, 1933, and *Six Restoration Plays,* ed. J. H. Wilson, Boston, 1959.

Useful critical studies of Restoration drama in general include Bonamy Dobrée's brilliant essays in *Restoration Comedy,* Oxford, 1924, and *Restoration Tragedy,* Oxford, 1929; Kathleen M. Lynch's *The Social Mode of Restoration Comedy,* New York, 1926; A. C. Sprague's history of *Beaumont and Fletcher on the Restoration Stage,* Cambridge, Mass., 1926; Hazelton Spencer's detailed discussion of Shakespearean adaptations in *Shakespeare Improved,* Cambridge, Mass., 1927 (re-issued, New York, 1963); Elizabeth L. Mignon's *Crabbed Age and Youth: The Old Men and Women in the*

Restoration Comedy of Manners, Durham, N. C., 1947; John Harrington Smith's *The Gay Couple in Restoration Comedy,* Cambridge, Mass., 1948; J. H. Wilson's *The Court Wits of the Restoration,* Princeton, 1948; and Thomas H. Fujimura's stimulating *The Restoration Comedy of Wit,* Princeton, 1952. L. C. Knight's, in "Restoration Comedy: The Reality and the Myth," *Explorations,* London, 1946, arguing that Restoration comedy is "insufferably dull," started a debate which is still going on. See Clifford Leech, "Restoration Comedy: The Earlier Phase," *Essays in Criticism,* I, 1951; F. W. Bateson, "Second Thoughts: II, L. C. Knights and Restoration Comedy," *Essays in Criticism,* VII, 1957; John Wain, "Restoration Comedy and Its Modern Critics," *Preliminary Essays,* London, 1957; and P. F. Vernon, "Marriage of Convenience and the Moral Code of Restoration Comedy," *Essays in Criticism,* XII, 1962.

Books and articles about individual dramatists or plays are legion. For Aphra Behn see George Woodcock, *The Incomparable Aphra,* New York, 1948, and a recent biographical study, W. J. Cameron's *New Light on Aphra Behn,* Auckland, N. Z., 1961. F. D. P. Senior included an edition of *The Careless Husband* in *The Life and Times of Colley Cibber,* London, 1928. For another consideration see Richard H. Barker's *Mr. Cibber of Drury Lane,* New York, 1939. The best biography of Congreve is that by John C. Hodges, *William Congreve, the Man,* New York, 1941. See also Kathleen M. Lynch, *A Congreve Gallery,* Cambridge, Mass., 1951, and Jean Gagen, "Congreve's Mirabell and the Ideal of the Gentleman," *PMLA,* LXXIX, 4, 1964.

George Saintsbury's *Dryden,* London, 1881, has been outmoded by C. E. Ward's *The Life of John Dryden,* Chapel Hill, N. C., 1963. Useful critical studies include Mark Van Doren's *John Dryden,* New York, 1946; Frank H. Moore's *The Nobler Pleasure,* Chapel Hill, N. C., 1963, and Arthur C. Kirsch's *Dryden's Heroic Dramas,* Princeton, 1965, an excellent study of the tragedies. For recent critical articles see especially Scott C. Osborne, "Heroical Love in Dryden's Heroic Drama," *PMLA,* LXXIII, 5, 1958, and Jean Gagen, "Love and Honor in Dryden's Heroic Plays," *PMLA,* LXXVII, 3, 1962.

For the background of libertinism in relation to Etherege, see Dale Underwood, *Etherege and the Seventeenth-Century Comedy of Manners,* New Haven, 1957. See also Arthur Sherbo, "Sir Fopling

Flutter and Beau Hewitt," *MLN*, LXIV, 1949. Farquhar's life and times were described by Willard Connely in *Young George Farquhar*, London, 1949, and R. G. Ham, in *Otway and Lee*, New Haven, 1931, combined two brief lives.

The best full-length study of Otway is Aline M. Taylor's *Next to Shakespeare*, Durham, N. C., 1950. For a selection of useful articles, see J. R. Moore, "Contemporary Satire in Otway's *Venice Preserved*," *PMLA*, XLIII, 1, 1928; R. E. Hughes, "'Comic Relief' in Otway's *Venice Preserved*," *N&Q*, n. s. 5, no. 2, 1958; and W. H. McBurney, "Otway's Tragic Muse Debauched: Sensuality in *Venice Preserved*," *JEGP*, LVIII, 3, 1959.

Shadwell, a much neglected dramatist, has received full attention only from Albert S. Borgman in *Thomas Shadwell, His Life and Comedies*, New York, 1928. Willard Connely made Wycherley the subject of a popular biography, *Brawny Wycherley*, New York, 1930. Recent significant articles are by Alexander H. Chorney, "Wycherley's Manly Reinterpreted," *Essays Critical and Historical Dedicated to Lily B. Campbell*, Berkeley, Cal., 1950, and K. M. Rogers, "Fatal Inconsistency: Wycherley and *The Plain-Dealer*," *ELH*, XXVIII, 1, 1961.

Index

* * *